Evocative Qualitative Inquiry

Evocative Qualitative Inquiry explores academic research that evokes vitality and life. It provides a road map into integrating the personal with professional to engage in intrinsically meaningful forms of inquiry.

The book centres on the key considerations of engaging in evocative forms of writing in the academy. It depicts academic inquiry as an embodied process that is captured and understood through rhythm and resonance. It relays how pleasurable, sensory, and rhythmic forms of inquiry can engender a sense of timelessness, expansiveness, growth, and generativity. *Evocative Qualitative Inquiry* relates the challenges that may arise from following this less trodden academic inquiry path. It conveys the importance of faith and courage in forging one's own unique and authentic writing voice. The book concludes with an analogy of a poker game to illustrate how all academic writers possess the embodied capacity to write vibrant words that evoke. Finally, each chapter ends with reflection questions and activities to help readers practice the skills of writing evocatively.

This book will be a valuable guide for those seeking evocative writing techniques to engage in vibrant forms of academic research. It is primarily written for academics who desire to learn more about creative, poetic, and embodied writing methodologies.

Joanne Yoo is Senior Lecturer at the School of International Studies and Education at the University of Technology Sydney (UTS). She currently teaches in UTS's secondary teacher education programs. Joanne's main research interests include writing as inquiry methodologies that involve the embodied, poetic, and evocative.

Developing Traditions in Qualitative Inquiry

Series Editors: Jasmine Brooke Ulmer and James Salvo
Wayne State University

The Developing Traditions in Qualitative Inquiry series invites scholars to share novel and innovative work in accessible ways, ways such that others might discover their own paths, too. In acknowledging who and what have respectively influenced our work along the way, this series encourages thoughtful engagements with approaches to inquiry – ones that are situated within ongoing scholarly conversations. Neither stuck in tradition nor unaware of it, volumes make new scholarly contributions to qualitative inquiry that attend to what's shared across disciplines and methodological approaches. By design, qualitative inquiry is a tradition of innovation in and of itself, one aimed at the target of justice.

From multiple perspectives and positionalities, concise volumes in this series (20,000 to 50,000 words) strengthen and grow the qualitative community by developing inquiry traditions as they should be developed: inclusively, diversely, and together.

For more information about the series or proposal guidelines, please write the Series Editors at jasmine.ulmer@wayne.edu and salvo@wayne.edu.

Other volumes in this series include

Writing and Unrecognized Academic Labor
The Rejected Manuscript
James M. Salvo

Centering Diverse Bodyminds in Critical Qualitative Inquiry
Edited by Jessica Nina Lester & Emily A. Nusbaum

Evocative Qualitative Inquiry
Writing and Research Through Embodiment and the Poetic
Joanne Yoo

For a full list of titles in this series, please visit www.routledge.com/Developing-Traditions-in-Qualitative-Inquiry/book-series/DTQI

Evocative Qualitative Inquiry

Writing and Research Through
Embodiment and the Poetic

Joanne Yoo

Routledge
Taylor & Francis Group

LONDON AND NEW YORK

First published 2022
by Routledge
2 Park Square, Milton Park, Abingdon, Oxon OX14 4RN

and by Routledge
605 Third Avenue, New York, NY 10158

Routledge is an imprint of the Taylor & Francis Group, an informa business

© 2022 Joanne Yoo

British Library Cataloguing-in-Publication Data
A catalogue record for this book is available from the British Library

Library of Congress Cataloging-in-Publication Data
A catalog record for this book has been requested

ISBN: 978-1-0321-4568-6 (hbk)
ISBN: 978-1-0321-4572-3 (pbk)
ISBN: 978-1-0032-3998-7 (ebk)

DOI: 10.4324/9781003239987

Typeset in Times New Roman
by Apex CoVantage, LLC

Contents

Preface

To 'know' something is a strange concept. It is one of those things that disappear the moment you begin looking for it. Our search for knowledge, at best, can appear like seeking a pot of gold at the bottom of a rainbow. And yet, knowledge, *real* knowledge, is elusive, because it unfolds in a lived moment. In other words, to know is to live, and to know well is to live a vibrant life.

Evocative Qualitative Inquiry contemplates this fundamental link between inquiry and life and examines what it means to draw us closer to the *truth* and *beauty* of what it means to 'know.' This book challenges readers to integrate how they live into how they write in the academy, and vice versa. It asserts that to know well, or write well, is indeed about learning how to live a magical life.

Acknowledgements

I thank my beautiful boys for all their love and joy. Thank you, Jasmine and James, the editors of this book series, for their wonderful support. I also thank my colleagues who provided feedback to early chapters of this book. Finally, my acknowledgements go to the evocative academic inquirers around the world, whose precious words have lit up my world.

1 Small beginnings

Why this book? Reflections on my academic career reveal that there are not many 'accidental' outcomes in life as our past plants the seed for the future. These seeds take root and grow slowly, nourished daily by our hopes and dreams, to eventually engineer our destinies. Such thoughts recently surfaced at a meeting for our newly restructured faculty where staff marvelled at their respective careers. They described themselves as falling into their work through a stroke of good fortune. I listened to their comments, thinking that their deepest desires had pulled them like a gravitational force. My yearning for vitality and creative self-expression has similarly drawn me to write *Evocative Qualitative Inquiry: Writing and Research Through Embodiment and the Poetic.* The thought that academic writing could be pleasurable and evocative had eluded me because it had been a painful and alienating process. From my earlier years of schooling, academic writing had meant adopting an impersonal and objective style of unyielding structures (Yoo, 2019e). These practices became further constricted with heavy layers of thick, impenetrable theory as I forged a career in academia. My naturally embodied writing style that felt intuitive did not seem *academic* enough, which meant that I never saw myself as a *proper* academic writer.

Evocative Qualitative Inquiry documents this journey of unlearning formal academic writing conventions and relearning ways to write vibrantly and authentically in academia. An intimate lens into the *writing as inquiry* terrain is as important as diverting from formal academic training can be challenging. Not only does it involve going against the flow of dominant norms and expectations regarding legitimate academic work, but non-mainstream academic approaches also present greater uncertainty. Creative inquiry methods are difficult to measure, which means that their value remains contested. Creative and evocative forms of academic inquiry do not conform to the conventions of mainstream academic journals, which can further reduce the publication opportunities that can advance one's academic career. As a result, academic writers may adopt academia's rigid and

DOI: 10.4324/9781003239987-1

objective approach despite desiring more creative and intrinsically meaningful inquiry modes.

The terms 'academic' and 'academia' themselves embody the positivist and objectivist structures of mainstream academic work. The *Merriam-Webster Dictionary* (n.d.-a) defines an 'academic' as someone who is "learned but inexperienced in practical matters" and who "conform[s] to the traditions or rules of a school or an official academy." Academic work is associated with learned fields of scientific theory and its intellectual rules, rather than the trusted 'truths' of practical experience. The term 'academy' further suggests that authority is held within the "established opinion widely accepted as valid in a particular field" (Merriam-Webster, n.d.-b). Legitimacy is accordingly positioned within academia's canonical gate-keeping structures of positivist discourses, and we may risk exclusion and marginalisation by venturing outside its norms.

Evocative Qualitative Inquiry presents a departure from the omniscient academic voice of scientific rationalism (Richardson, 2001). It explores alternate creative academic inquiry paths that embody Richardson's (2002a) provocative questions of, "What to write? How to write? For whom to write?" (p. 416). These questions create spaces for vibrant and pleasurable inquiry forms by bridging the superficial divide between academic and creative writing. To embrace the personal is to acknowledge that *all* writing is framed by our subjectivities (Norton, 2013). Murray (1986) urges academic writers to discern and to acknowledge their own personal voice, declaring, "We are lucky to have a vocation of scholarship, a calling. But who is calling? Ourselves . . . write for yourself – try to figure out what you want to say rather than what other people want" (p. 147). To uncover voice is to write to "nam[e] our reality," instead of adopting the frameworks of others; writing becomes an act of affirmation and life, rather than a mechanical and instrumental process (Colyar, 2009, p. 425). Our writing reveals our subjective lens on the world. This lens can be seen through the different meanings associated with terms, such as temperature and heat. Temperature is measured by Fahrenheit or degrees, whilst heat is often associated with feelings of warmth (Barone & Eisner, 2012). Sensations of heat are therefore felt subjectively, whilst temperature is determined by objective measurements. Through exploring these various shades of subjective meaning, we can become immersed in rich nuanced worlds.

We write evocatively to assert our presence and to affirm our own perceptions. By acknowledging our subjective lens, we become both the subject and mode of research (Goodall, 2001; Pelias, 2005). Richardson (2001) describes such research as a form of *writing as inquiry* as the writing process itself becomes our primary means of research. To write evocatively is to focus on the *hows* as well as the *whats*. Evocative inquiry defines academic writing as a way of *coming into* knowing rather than simply being a means to an end. Richardson (2001) highlights this shifting orientation as she describes her formal academic writing training, stating, "I was taught, though, as perhaps you were, too, not to write until I knew what I wanted to say, until my points were organized and outlined" (p. 35). *Evocative Qualitative Inquiry* depicts knowing as an unfolding lived moment that is shaped by the writer's unique lived experiences (Norton, 2013). To write evocatively is to subvert dominant positivist and instrumental norms and to engage the creative and aesthetic to deepen understanding.

Writing evocatively embodies the postmodernist view that multiple versions of *truth* exist as knowledge is 'constructed' within a particular paradigm (Ellis, Adams, & Bochner, 2011). Examining and articulating one's beliefs about academic inquiry creates opportunities to question why we think and act the way we do, since our values and beliefs become concrete as we externalise them. To write and inquire evocatively is to generate a manifesto of intrinsically meaningful forms of academic inquiry. Williams (2020) defines this process of articulating what one knows as a manifesto, relaying how creative writers may write to *manifest* their "mysterious/mystical" inner workings (p. 72). He believes that manifestos "enliven and focus a writer's power, demarcate a territory, make an argument, and contribute to the ongoing debate about who we are as writers" (p. 78). Manheimer (1999) asserts that manifesting intent is to live a deliberate life of freedom, declaring:

> The ability to act with deliberateness – a word implying liberation, freedom and libra, the constellation of the scales, justice – must be refined over time. . . . To choose well and wisely how you want to conduct your life, to act from a compelling sense of what is yours to do, is at the heart of what it means to live deliberately.
>
> (p. 136)

Evocative Qualitative Inquiry presents one manifesto of writing vibrantly and deliberately in the academy. It traces my journey of diverting from the well-trodden path of mainstream academic writing discourse to merge the personal with the professional (Yoo, 2017, 2018, 2019a). It further describes the steps taken to discover voice through crafting rhythm, uncovering essence, and generating resonance. This book relates the challenges of undertaking such a journey and highlights how faith is required to venture into the spaces of the *not yet*. Each chapter begins with a discussion of one aspect of evocative inquiry, such as resonance, voice, and time. The chapters conclude with reflection questions and practical writing activities to help readers explore the writing style or principles introduced. The terms 'evocative inquiry' and 'evocative writing' are used interchangeably as *writing as inquiry* is inherently evocative as vibrant understanding is *evoked* through the writing process itself. The terms 'poetic,' 'embodied,' and 'evocative writing' and 'inquiry' are also used synonymously to represent a growing sphere of qualitative writing that is lyric, rhythmic, and evokes a highly sensual and affective response.

What does it mean to evoke?

The road to evocative inquiry first became visible when I sought alternatives to rigid academic writing styles that alienated and disengaged. Saldaña (2014) expresses a similar dissatisfaction with mainstream academic discourses devoid of authentic language, stating:

> OK. Now . . . you see . . . this is another one of those things that some people seem to put a lotta stock in: "conceptual framework," "theoretical perspective," "epistemological foundations," "methodological premises" – whatever. How 'bout me just sayin' what it really is and what I really mean: This is where I'm comin' from.
>
> (p. 977)

Academics may adopt overly complex and instrumental styles as they become confused about what it means to write 'academically.' Believing authority to lie outside of themselves, they may conform to dominant mainstream academic conventions (Hooks, 2000). Such confusion led me to appropriate the conventions of positivist writing paradigms, despite how they negated my embodied ways of thinking and being. After years of feeling alienated from myself, I began seeking more vibrant, meaningful, and enjoyable writing forms such as the poetic and embodied. Writing evocatively became my way of "bypass[ing] the homogenized scientific ways of knowing . . . demystif[y] claims to textual authority" and resolving my dissatisfaction around simple and reductionist thinking (Richardson, 2002b, p. 417). These transformations could occur as my beliefs about legitimacy and authority shifted from external to internal discourses. Writing *about* and *from* my embodied sensations helped me to explore and express my lived experiences in intimate, pleasurable, and authentic ways. The impact of this shift was profound. Not only did writing become more enjoyable, the more enjoyable it became, the more I wrote and published (Yoo, 2018).

Evocative forms of writing and inquiry animate and inspire. To 'evoke' is to "call up or produce (memories, feelings, etc.), elicit or draw forth, produce, or suggest through artistry and imagination a vivid impression of reality" (Dictionary.com, n.d.-a, para. 1). To 'evoke' is to elicit a powerful response, highlighted by the Latin term ēvocāre, which means 'to call forth,' and its stem, 'vocāre' (Dictionary.com, n.d.-a). It involves bringing forth hidden meaning to activate its rich potential for animation, being, and purpose, and to seek deeper or higher sources of meaning that become a vocation or life's purpose. A *calling* is evoked when you find yourself so deeply moved that you become wholly immersed in your work. Evocative writers find their calling craft deeply aesthetic words that triggers the imagination and transports readers into a timeless and expansive realm. The evocative harnesses this power to generate fresh perspectives or new ways to *read* and experience the world (Eisner, 2012), initiating new combinations that have not yet been considered (Langer, 2005). Not surprisingly, once I experienced the pleasure and vitality of writing and inquiring evocatively, it was difficult to consider any other way.

Autoethnographers often engage in evocative writing to inquire into their lived experience. In particular, Ellis and Bochner have played a significant role in highlighting the evocative as a methodological concept in the context of autoethnographic writing – and living – especially in their book *Evocative Autoethnography: writing lives and telling stories* (Bochner & Ellis, 2016). Qualitative researchers are greatly indebted to this methodological contribution that reinforces how writing about life is to capture its vibrance. My writing here wishes to extend this work and develop the concept beyond the autoethnographic. It attempts to bring the evocative into the context of research writing in general, and to explore evocative writing forms such as the embodied and poetic. It provides further insight into the experience of writing evocatively in the academy by describing the joyful states of timelessness, the authenticity of voice, and the importance of faith and of staying in the present time.

Evocative writers *evoke* richer and deeper forms of understanding by questioning and repositioning their sense-making frames. They explore diffractive possibilities of knowing by continuing to ask, 'why and what else?' They can break down fixed frames of perception by not only asking about *what* they know, but *how* they know. Such questions can evoke a novel and affective response as the knower continues to challenge and expand their knowing by exploring untapped avenues of thought (Davies, 2017). Academics who question what it means to know through writing evocatively can increase their attunement to what is authentic, dynamic, and resonating. Their writing style reflects their animating presence, giving insight into who they are and how they occupy the world (Clough, 1996). The process of writing itself becomes a rich topic for inquiry as academics can explore more vivid, authentic, and pleasurable ways of expressing *what* and *how* they know.

Evocative writing celebrates the personal, unique, and embodied lens. It acknowledges that academic writing cannot be separated from the writer's selfhood since words come alive through the author's *presence*. This presence attributes their words a sense of authenticity, vitality, and internal locus of authority. Alternatively, to deny personhood is to draw an incomplete picture as research is separated from the knower's lens or frameworks for knowing. Huxley (1959) presents this view through the three poles of writing, asserting, "There is a pole of the personal and the autobiographical; there is the pole of the objective, the factual, the concrete-particular; and there is the pole of the abstract-universal," describing how writers can achieve a state of timelessness by writing from all three poles (v–vii). Writing authentically through the senses is to become whole and undiminished, as all the separate parts come together to form a complete and coherent picture (Merriam-Webster, n.d.-c). This wholehearted or holistic approach manifests when the mind, heart, and senses are aligned through affect-laden and embodied language. Writing and inquiring from an integrated self constitutes freedom as the research process brings us closer to ourselves.

Evoking mystery

Evocative forms of inquiry embody an openness and receptivity to tacit and embodied understandings (Yoo, 2021b). Antonio Damasio (2000) describes how our earliest or 'core' sense of selfhood pre-exists language. It is this "felt, bodily sense of self" that reconnects us with similar aspects of our experiences (as cited in Nicholls, 2009, p. 173). Writing that *evokes* is fluid enough to encompass *felt and bodily* sense; it can capture the felt sense as it abandons predetermined structures and persists through the "obscurity and darkness of uncertainty" (Pallasmaa, 2009, p. 108). The journey itself becomes the revelation as we follow a trail of insights to uncover the deeper recesses of hidden meaning. Murray (1984) depicts such writers as "rationalisers of accident" because they come to their writing through the act of writing itself (p. 1). Murray (1982) highlights this creative potential of writing, relaying how writers can manoeuvre themselves intuitively through the obscure and muddy sense-making process to "follow thinking that has not yet become thought," as well as by reading "patterns and designs – sketches of possible relationships between pieces of information or fragments of rhetoric or language" (p. 141).

Evocative writers consequently become explorers or mapmakers who follow this first hint of meaning or "effervescent buzz" to uncover hidden meaning (Dewsbury, 2014, p. 148). They tap into deeper meanings by writing to uncover undercurrents of vitality. Effervescent writing tingles, refreshes and awakens, and emerges from effervescent encounters that, "touch something deep inside you, [which] makes you stop and question yourself, the way you're living your life, urges you to scrutinize contradictions, inconsistencies and incongruities, makes your blind spots visible" (Bochner, 2009,

p. 162). These encounters contain a hidden story that demands to be told. We become receptive to such stories through a keen sense of curiosity and receptivity, and a rich attunement to life (Rodgers & Raider-Roth, 2006). Our openness and curiosity drive us to seek questions rather than answers, so that we can enjoy a continuous unravelling of surprises (Cloutier, 2016).

Evocative writers embrace openness, curiosity, and a heightened sensitivity. To write evocatively is to grasp fleeting and spontaneous intuitions that emerge when we are immersed in a state of wonder. Dewsbury (2014) settles on the word 'apprehensive' to highlight how opportunities unfold within uncertain spaces. Rather than dwelling on the fearfulness of not knowing, he frames 'apprehension' through a state of possibilities, "to apprehend, but not be certain; to be apprehended, to arrest, to be arrested, to be caught dumbfounded in the flow of someone else, something else, a breeze, a warm glow of sunlight effect: to understand, practically, not intellectually" (p. 148). To 'apprehend' is to be open to uncertainty and to grasp something just out of hand's reach; it is to catch a hint of meaning to pursue 'felt' meanings. To evoke potential is to unravel the 'not yet,' rather than reproducing a predetermined output or product and to "develop and exploit the surprise that was only a hint, a revealing snap of a twig, a shadow in the bush before the writer pounced" (Murray, 1984, p. 6). The mind that apprehends is highly attuned to the evocative and can catch snippets of details to "enter into the skin of others" (Murray, 1982, p. 14). To evoke is to coax others into the wonder of unfolding possibility.

Overview of the chapters

Chapter 1 introduces the reasons why academics should write evocatively. *Small beginnings* describes my journey of exploring qualitative writing forms, such as the embodied and poetic. Evocative forms of inquiry differ from mainstream academic writing and research conventions as they merge the professional and personal realms. The personal lens adds authenticity, authority, and vibrance by animating words with presence. This chapter conveys how an evocative inquiry approach involves embracing the rich mystery that unfolds in the liminal spaces of the *not yet*. Chapter 1 provides an overview of the book's chapters and concludes with questions on researching and writing evocatively in the academy.

Evocative forms of writing and inquiry evoke the senses by drawing on our embodied ways of knowing. Chapter 2 describes the theoretical frameworks of the *inscribed* and *lived* body to highlight the primacy and authority of the body. *The body that evokes* depicts how embodiment drives reflexivity and social justice through providing a voice for those who have been marginalised by mainstream academic writing discourses. It highlights the skilful, colourful, and evocative language of embodied prose that captures the tacit and intuitive sensations of the body. This chapter presents techniques for replacing dry and sterile academic writing approaches with rich sensory, visceral, and evocative language. It includes illustrations of embodied writing to demonstrate how sensual words can stir affect and bring words to life.

Chapter 3 highlights the essence, resonance, and expansivity of evocative forms of inquiry, such as poetic writing. *Essence, resonance, and the expansivity of the poetic* conveys how poetic words that evoke the senses can conjure vivid images that allow readers to deeply inhabit an encounter. Such rhythmic words resonate as they harmonise with a reader's tacit ways of knowing; they are powerfully seductive and make us surrender to the pleasures of evoking the senses. Beautiful configurations of words also help us to consider our encounters in new and insightful ways. This chapter provides excerpts of poetic writing to demonstrate how writers can seduce and lull readers into a deeper understanding. It depicts evocative inquiry as a form of communion, in which writers and readers dwell within a shared encounter. Chapter 3 concludes with activities for practicing artful and poetic forms that relay essence and cultivate resonance.

Evocative inquiry cultivates a sense of timelessness. Chapter 4 explores the expansivity evoked by aesthetic writing forms that connect writers and readers with what is *lived* and *felt*. Timelessness is likened to an altered state of consciousness, in which individuals become so immersed in an activity that they lose awareness of self and time. Academic writers become equally engrossed in their work as they write evocatively to cultivate a sense of flow and pleasure. Rhythm and resonance help readers to harmonise with a writer's thoughts so that they can experience a timeless space. *Crafting timelessness through aesthetic writing* explores how the aesthetic can transcend barriers and borders to enrich and expand understanding.

Growth and generativity emerge from evocative forms of inquiry. Chapter 5 relates how evocative modes of research and writing trigger growth as they animate words with feeling and presence. *Growth and generativity through narratives* focuses on this generative potential through examining the textuality and intertextuality of evocative writing. It describes the parallels between living and writing evocatively, such as a coherent structure and an open-ended form. The evocative is conveyed as the essence of a vibrant authentic academic text, as well as an intrinsically meaningful life. This chapter explores how evocative inquiry can help academics carve out vibrant research trajectories by equipping them with the colourful words that encompass the tacit and mysterious. Evocatively crafted words are depicted as having a powerful impact as it evokes our rich capacity for growth and generativity.

Chapter 6 describes how evocative, vibrant, and pleasurable writing embodies *voice*. *Hearing voice* presents evocative writing as a way of accessing personal and natural modes of knowing and expression, since writers can powerfully engage readers by speaking from their intimate voice. The reading and writing process becomes a mutually reciprocal encounter as the writer engages readers through dwelling within a shared moment. Evocative inquiry cultivates an authentic connection between the writer and reader since the writer imbues his or her words with their presence to be intimately known. Chapter 6 presents writing as an act of creation that reflects the creator's craftsmanship or voice. It concludes with exercises that can help academic writers relay their animating voice through equally vibrant words.

Despite the pleasure and intrinsic meaning derived from writing evocatively, such a creative approach can be challenging to adopt in academia as it entails writing against the grain. Chapter 7 accordingly depicts the importance of courage and faith to pursue evocative forms of inquiry. Courage is required to oppose mainstream academic writing conventions that objectify and minimise. Faith also motivates us to persist despite the possibility of rejection. Pursuing the evocative requires faith because it involves persisting through the uncertainty to uncover the *not yet*. The path to evocative inquiry is unknown, which means that there are no predetermined steps to follow or a final destination in sight. Faith, courage, and a strong desire for authentic and rich forms of inquiry are crucial for overcoming our doubts and accessing the aesthetic, pleasurable, and intrinsically meaningful. *Faith and evocative inquiry* depicts what it means to persist on the journey of evocative inquiry.

The final chapter provides an overview of the previous themes and concludes with a call for academics to write and inquire evocatively. *Writing in the here and now* revisits the concepts of embodiment, rhythm, resonance, generativity, time, and voice through an analogy of a poker game. The poker game metaphor illustrates how academics can engage in evocative inquiry in the present as they already possess the rich embodied experiences to write meaningfully, vibrantly, and impactfully. This metaphor reveals how academic writers can capture the richness of knowing by tapping into the *here and now* and entering the liminal space of the *not yet*.

Reflecting on your journey into evocative inquiry

1 First thoughts

We are often so busy trying to get somewhere that we don't stop to ponder where we are going or why we are trying to get there. This was the case in the early stages of my academic career when I was desperately trying to acquire tenure. It was difficult to slow down and contemplate the *whys* as I was too busy trying to secure my future. Regardless of the stages in our academic careers, it is important to take stock of where we are going and why we are going there, otherwise our journey may be wasted. Take this opportunity to think about your academic writing journey. Which words, images, or metaphors come to mind as you think about your research? What might these words or images signify and why do you think they come to mind?

2 Self-introduction

Through the process of writing this book, I realised that it was a manifesto about a journey towards writing evocatively in the academy. The writing process itself was particularly challenging as I desired to find words that evoked vibrant life. Consider what your academic writing says about you. Describe what your subject matter and writing style reflect about your beliefs and values about your work. Try writing a brief manifesto of your academic writing approach.

3 Evocative inquiry

This first chapter introduced you to the topic of evocative qualitative inquiry. When you think of the word *evocative*, what thoughts come to mind? Have you associated the evocative with academic inquiry, why or why not? Do you consider yourself to be an evocative academic writer? (Save this piece of writing so you can return to it after you have finished reading this book).

4 Reflecting on the journey

A journey often reveals more than the destination itself. The chapters in this book present the various forks I have undertaken on the evocative qualitative inquiry path. A map of the steps I have taken emerged through the process of writing this book. Describe your academic writing journey so far. What have been your major influences and turning points? Contemplate how these influences and turning points have come together to set you on your particular path.

5 Finding models to follow

I have gravitated towards poetic and embodied writers in my academic inquiry journey as I find their work pleasurable and enjoyable to read. Their writing style resonates and provides a road map for me to follow. In this book, you will find multiple references to their work. Who are your favourite academic writers? What do you enjoy about their writing style and how does your writing mirror or differ from those of these writers?

6 Writing aspirations

When we embark on a journey into uncertain spaces, it can be helpful to visualise the end. Imagining the end can help us to maintain our focus on our desired goal and not get side-tracked. Think about your goals for your academic writing career. What do you want to write about and how do you want to write about it? Write a letter to yourself after having spent an academic career researching and writing according to your deepest aspirations. What would you like to say to yourself at this point in time?

7 Coming into your writing

Evocative qualitative inquiry evokes. It evokes new life and understandings, which trigger further insight and inquiry. How do you come into your subject matter? Think about the ways that you engage in new academic writing projects. Where do you get your inspiration? Write expressively about where you think your ideas come from.

2   The body that *evokes*

Noticing the body

It is late evening,
and you have just opened that paper,
you started,
a year ago,
that has been buried,
under an endless stream of tasks.

This evening,
with only a couple of hours remaining,
you decide to revisit,
this distant memory.
But the moment you click open the document,
your mind feels heavy,
and your eyelids begin to droop.

You read the first line over and over,
unable to comprehend its meaning.
Disconcerted,
and frustrated,
anxiety pervades.

You are aware in that moment,
deep in your bones,
and in the tired buzz behind your eyes,
that the body speaks.

The body's primacy becomes evident when we explore how we make sense
of the world. At first *touch*, we realise how we record our moments through
what we see, hear, taste, smell, and touch. These raw sensations reveal how

DOI: 10.4324/9781003239987-2

we locate ourselves in place and time through our bodies, as we process the world "directly as an embodied and sensory activity without being turned into concepts or even entering the sphere of consciousness" (Pallasmaa, 2009, p. 118). What we glean from our senses is pieced together to construct our evolving schemas for interpretation. In academia, tension arises when our tacit and sensory ways of knowing conflict with more dominant positivist and quantitative discourses. With the 'publish or perish' mandate, the pressure to conform to mainstream academic writing styles intensifies so we curb what feels natural to publish our work. To overcome this increasingly instrumental focus, academic writers may reclaim their writing through more authentic, instinctive, and pleasurable forms. *But where do they start?*

It was easy to disown the body as an academic writer. From the early years of my formal academic writing training, I learnt to swallow the body's sensations and to adopt the objectivist third person voice. The gap between the personal and professional grew wider when I added dense layers of theory to validate my words, convincing myself that the body's intelligence had no place in academic writing. This was until physical changes, such as illness, began to impact my performance so that I could no longer ignore the body (Yoo, 2019d). Other embodied states, such as pregnancy, derailed daily rhythms and communicated unwanted messages of unavailability. These physical changes increasingly revealed that the body was a primary means of being in the world. I became more and more curious about how my academic peers responded to their bodies. They composed words over screens, eyes glazed, and spines curved; their bodies becoming diminished as they lived a life of the mind. I also noticed how my colleagues would talk about their physical frailty in hushed tones, fearful of disclosing vulnerability and too busy *getting on with things*. References to sick bodies were absent even though some had battled very serious, life-threatening ailments. I felt as if we were all in denial of the body's importance, despite the ways that physical fatigue and illness had derailed our lives.

My interest in the body was planted early on in life, first coming to my attention during childhood. I became aware of what it meant to live as an Asian kid in a predominantly white Anglo-Saxon school of fair-skinned, blond, red-haired, or brown-eyed children. My ethnic body felt *marked* due to its differences (Yoo, 2020a). The contrasting textures of our hair were immediately noticeable, and although I was not fully conscious of the reasons why, I knew that I wanted to trade my coarse and wiry black hair with their soft and shimmering locks. These feelings of separateness returned after entering academia as I observed eyes gravitating towards me, taking note of my dark hair and olive-coloured skin. *What's her story?* I could almost hear them ask. The lack of bodies with a similar colouring had made mine unique, suggesting that there was a story to be told. Despite wanting to blend in and to feel the comfort of anonymity, I could not trade my physical features. Many years of being observed in this way heightened my sensitivity to the body and positioned it at the forefront of consciousness (Yoo, 2020a).

As an academic writer, I felt a similar dissonance between external expectations and personal desires. My embodied ways of knowing clashed with positivist and objectivist academic structures, as like my physical body, my writing style did not conform to dominant norms. The embodied knowledge that I possessed as a middle-aged woman of Asian heritage, appeared to be at odds with the scientific, disembodied, Eurocentric, and masculine forms of knowledge represented by older White male bodies (Wilcox, 2009). Attempting to write from a voice or body that was the polar opposite to my own was like trying to speak in a foreign language. Saldaña (2014) satirically highlights the need to write in ways that reflects who we are, writing:

> My position? I'm right here in front of you. Look at me: I'm a 59-year-old man with a white beard. Gay leather bear, Hispanic, a touch of Cajun (in spirit, not by blood), with a little bit of bad-ass biker in me, and a proud dash of redneck-wannabe. Overweight, asthmatic, a little arthritis; I don't complain much, I git [sic] by.
>
> (p. 976)

This dominant academic language sat awkwardly on my tongue and I spoke it without finesse, trying to adopt its rules to extreme rigidity, despite losing myself in the process. Its rigid structures created an atmosphere of objectivity and distance. It conflicted with how I thought, felt, and moved, giving no hint to who I was and how I desired to be.

The *inscribed* and the *lived* body

Embodied writing presented a means of escaping such dissonance. The path to emancipation became visible when reading Grosz's (1994) *Volatile bodies: Toward a corporeal feminism* and encountering the notions of the *lived* and *inscribed* body. Grosz (1994) defines the *lived* body as how the body is physically experienced through the senses of taste, touch, smell, hearing, and sight. The *inscribed* body, on the other hand, relates to the bodily cultural markers that hold implicit value-laden messages and shape our understanding. The *inscribed* and *lived* body are intrinsically linked, since the body is etched with markers of age, gender, and ethnicity that colour how we view the world and vice versa. We encounter the world through the *lived* body or our physical senses, whilst the raw and lived data is interpreted by the *inscribed* body or the value-laden physical features that mark our bodies. Moreover, our identification with certain bodily markers may cause us to think and behave in socially prescribed ways. We may carry out certain actions due to our culture, gender, and age, believing that this is how we should be and act. Grosz's (1994) definitions highlight how our bodies can determine how we encounter the world. For instance, I could see how the *lived* body impacted my perceptions when I became ill. When my body felt broken, consciousness would fragment and my writing would become disjointed, as I wrote, "My physical senses help me to capture and depict the fragmented mind that registers the body. It manifests as an incoherent layering of sentences of tired stream of consciousness; it is a window to a life in disarray" (Yoo, 2019d, p. 1104). The ways my physical encounters shaped my words revealed how understanding was fundamentally embodied.

Embodied and subjective ways of knowing have unfortunately been discredited by traditional academic discourses that prioritise the intellect over the body (Freedman & Holmes, 2012). Positivist discourses devalue the body for being less concrete, unpredictable, unsophisticated, inferior to the mind and too "personal, immediate and messy" to constitute "acceptable knowledge" (Tangenberg & Kemp, 2002, p. 11). They depict embodied forms of knowing as being less accurate and valid than logical and rational thinking. As an embodied academic writer, I consequently felt like a child who continued to draw on childish bodily ways of knowing (Grosz, 2005). These disembodied ways of knowing have been traced to Western academic practices that regard the body as being inferior to the mind. In other words, the body has been *inscribed* with markers that convey measures of value and worth, such as age, gender, and race. Sharp (2009) draws a connection between the body and culture, asserting that the body bears the colonial rationalist's beliefs that non-White races are more primitive, instinct-driven, and inferior to their mentally superior colonisers. He highlights how marginalised bodies carry certain cultural meanings that signify lower power levels since they do not possess the same markers as those associated with dominant discourse. Ellingson (2006) likewise depicts bodies as political sites of knowledge production as she discusses the privileges of her *white* body, stating how her *whiteness* became an "unearned social privilege" (p. 306) that enabled implicit acceptance from other healthcare professionals. She examines "the [forgotten] ontology of the body" and the ways that bodies can be "acculturated, psychologized, given identity, historical location, and agency" (Grosz, 2005, p. 2). Bhattacharya (2016) also relates how her dark skin associates her with "limited and mitigated, cross-cultural" speech, despite her resistance to "being a 'Third-World' broker of knowledge" (p. 316). Her writing resonated with me as I felt that my black hair, slanted eyes, and female body bore similar culturally loaded messages, and that my embodied ways of knowing were overshadowed by the rationalist thinking of more privileged bodies (Wilcox, 2009).

The *lived* body aligns with embodied and evocative forms of knowing and inquiry, suggesting that we know through the "modalities of taste, hearing, touch, pain, smell, sight and kinesthesia" and through the "moving body, the doing itself" (Farnell & Varela, 2008, p. 216). Deleuze (1988) explains how the process of *becoming* lies in the body's ability to affect and be affected. Bodily movement is closely related to the *affective* body, which positions the body as an organ that moves and feels (Massumi, 2002). In other words, bodies in motion are positive and affirmative as they are "defined by their relations and affects, opening up or closing down possibilities . . . in continuous movement and negotiation" (Coffey, 2012, p. 16). Deleuze (1988) construes bodies as "intensities, rather than entities" as they feel, interact, become, and move in practice or performance (p. 7). This movement of affect and intensities demonstrates expertise across a wide variety of human endeavours, as Pallasmaa (2009) writes:

> For the sportsman, craftsman, magician and artist alike, the seamless and unconscious collaboration of the eye, hand and mind is crucial. As the performance is gradually perfected, perception, action of the hand and thought lose their independence and turn into a singular and subliminally coordinated system of reaction and response.
>
> (p. 82)

Embodied writing gives expression to these vibrant bodily sensations, as Pelias (2016) declares, "I speak from the body . . . a scholarship attuned to the visceral and somatic. . . . I am my body speaking. I am a mind/body fully engaged" (p. 388). Cixous (1976) equally iterates how speaking *the body* is to assert oneself into the world and to create a textual sense of being. As she explains, "Woman must per herself into the text-as into the world and into history-by her own movement" (p. 875). The literature on embodiment reveals how we compose ourselves through the raw sensory material that is caught, interpreted, deconstructed, and constructed by the body (Merleau-Ponty, 1967). We can accordingly lose self-consciousness and experience positive emotion by becoming physically caught up in an activity. To *know* is to be animate and alive, as by becoming lost to bodily movement, we immerse ourselves in an affective and aesthetic process (Yoo & Loch, 2016). Embodied writing allows us to merge with our various bodily sensations and emotions, such as the heaviness of our legs and a quickening beat of the heart. These sensations demonstrate the tacit and embodied ways we engage the world.

What is embodied writing?

Significant topics emerge as we write freely about our bodily sensations, such as the sinking feeling in our gut, the tightness of our foreheads or the lightness of our feet. *What do these bodily reactions signify?* The heaviness in our stomachs may indicate a sense of dread or foreboding and tightness can convey stress and angst, whilst light footedness may suggest exuberance and delight. Our bodies reveal our thoughts and longings, many of which elude the conscious mind. By capturing the fleeting sensations that arise in the moment, we can remain whole and fully engaged in the *here and now*. Writing on an embodied level is to be equally in touch with ourselves. As Tuinamuana and Yoo (2020) ask, "Have we lost the ability to connect with ourselves? Have we lost touch with our emotions and our bodies?" (p. 1004). Through writing *from* and *of* the body, we can capture the full spectrum of human encounters from the extreme heights of ecstasy to the depths of sorrow. Pelias (2016) further asserts that we write the *personal* in embodied ways and become whole by connecting with our bodies, stating, "Writing the personal, I speak from the body . . . a scholarship attuned to the visceral and somatic. . . . I am my body speaking. I am a mind/body fully engaged" (p. 388). Merging our consciousness with the body's messages constitutes a process of entirety and completeness, which in turn allows us to speak from the depth of our being. These skilful, colourful, and evocative depictions of our bodily sensations can help close the gap between our accounts and actual experiences (Sparkes, 1996).

This chapter provides extracts of evocative writing to demonstrate embodied writing's visceral impact. These examples replace objective and highly structured academic prose with richly sensory, visceral, and evocative language that is acutely felt and expressed through the body. Pallasmaa (2012) expresses this rich awakening of the senses through a walk in a forest, as he writes:

> A walk through a forest is invigorating and healing due to the constant interaction of all sense modalities. . . . The eye collaborates with the

body and the other senses. One's sense of reality is strengthened and articulated by this constant interaction.

(p. 44)

Evocative academic writers attempt to express the affective and embodied knowing captured through the senses. One example of embodied writing that resonated deeply with me was Tillman's (2009) *Body and Bulimia Revisited: Reflections on "A Secret Life,"* which addresses the question, "When one takes the view from the trenches, what do embodied knowledges look like? How do we claim or even recognise bodily knowledges?" (Wilcox, 2009, p. 106). Her paper demonstrates how writing *about* and *from* your body is to bring someone into the intimate sphere of your private world. Tillman (2009) creates an intimate space by depicting her broken marriage in embodied and visceral terms, transforming readers into emotionally attuned and responsive individuals. My bodily responses mirrored Tillman's as her words brought me to my own embodied recollections of grief, "[as] a place inside of me expands. Reflexively, my body and spirit make[s] space for grief" when stories of trauma are heard (p. 101). Tillman (2009) is an *emotional historian*, who mirrors her mother's childhood to her siblings; she reveals the soft and hard experience of a separation, as she observes, "Laying my head upon his chest-his center, my center for 13 years – I absorb his scent and listen to him breathe. Everything around me – and in me – softens" (pp. 101–105). We experience her grief through her raw and visceral descriptions, breathing in the scent of a loved one that makes the tight edges fade away. Her embodied account contains rich sensory details that illustrate how experience is interpreted through our subjectivities (Cloutier, 2016). It reveals how we can become better emotional sense-makers through greater exposure to such vibrant, sensory, and evocative accounts.

   To write evocatively is to acknowledge that our sense of *being in the world* is fundamentally embodied. This means that the memories that shape our identities are encoded through our senses. Gorman (2018) illustrates this notion through a visceral account of caring for an aging ballerina when she was a young hospice nurse. She captures the regality of the time-worn dancer, as she writes, "Clear blue eyes belied her age and remained her only form of expressive connection. In the final throes of dementia, she remained almost haughty, aloof – a finely sculpted artist with a patrician nose and proud cheekbones" (p. 163). This former ballet dancer leaves Gorman (2018) with her last prized possessions of three gold bracelets, which Gorman does not accept as she believes to be unethical. Her understanding of ethics deepens over time by becoming reframed through relationships. As she relates, "On a more visceral level, full metabolism has been slower in coming. I am still digesting what these experiences teach" (p. 164). The emotional maturity she acquires through a long and fruitful career enables Gorman (2018) to describe the soul of nursing in visceral and embodied terms, where she reflects, "The great gratification of nursing arises within the context of the stripped-down, raw-to-the-bone relationship. It resides in moments of semi darkness when mortality looms large and passions rekindle briefly, sparked by human proximity" (p. 165). Her raw embodied language cuts into our consciousness, allowing us to contemplate her beautiful tale of honouring an aging ballerina's life.

Embodied writing can depict the full breadth of human experience. Examples of such raw writing remind us not to shy away from difficult topics, but to explore them instead for what they can teach us. In *Hospice 101*, Richardson (2011) uses embodied language to softly convey the topics of death and dying. She does not turn away from confronting her mortality as she asks, "How shall I spend my moments?" (p. 159). Instead, she tries to make sense of her beloved sister's death through depicting the cancer cells savagely attacking her body, as she writes, "She nods and puts my right hand on her upper intestine and the left one near her pubic bone. Beneath each hand I feel a hard rock, the size of my fist. I send healing thoughts through my arms, thoughts to remove her pain. I don't want her in pain" (Richardson, 2011, p. 160). Richardson (2011) relays her profound sense of loss through the details of her sister's cancer ravaged body, relating:

> For the next five days, I watch aides bathe Sarah with lotion. I see her entire body – bones, bruises, black spots, nipples hanging low without breast tissue, swollen pubis. She looks like an Auschwitz survivor. Dehydration and starvation toward death make us all look alike – our essential bones and skin and eyes that are wide, too protruded, too big for their sockets, bigger than our empty stomachs.
>
> (p. 161)

We write evocatively to faithfully depict our lived experiences. Richardson (2011) illustrates the significance of writing about difficult topics, displaying the "sensibility, imagination, technique" required "to make judgements about the feel and significance of particular" (Eisner, 2002, p. 32). She highlights how the body connects us to our shared human condition, reflecting on how we all look similar in the final stages of an illness. She draws our attention to the hope that pervades, recounting how her family concludes the memorial of her sister's death with a goodbye ceremony involving "six handmade ceramic spheres, each having a hollow space in its middle and each unique in coloration, shape, and heft. Each one was beautiful. Natural looking," as well as "hot-fudge ice-cream sundaes" that are eaten around a "round oak kitchen table" (Richardson, 2011, pp. 164–165). Hope stirs through the taste of soft light vanilla, the solid touch of the oak table and the warm memories of our loved ones.

Words imbued with the physical senses evoke lived experience. Lindauer (2005) writes how words capture the motion of our sensations as he describes the link between creative writing and physiognomy:

> Letters, words, phrases, and sentences are physical and sensory stimuli composed of straight, slanted, and curved lines of various shapes, forms, sizes, lengths, and spatialities. . . . Words do not lie inertly on a page but resonate with a rhythm and flow that "sing," "pulsate," "shine," and reverberate like a song.
>
> (p. 122)

Embodied writing deeply immerses us in an experience so that we can be "physically present on the page, at hand, ready to listen, having been drawn into the re-enactment – in the flesh so to speak – ready to encounter something new, freshly (or perhaps fleshly)" (Rendle-Short, 2015, p. 98). Todres and Galvin (2008) equally propose that embodied writing can bring phenomena to life, since words that "are faithful to the phenomenon in all its complexity, sense and texture" can convey the felt sense (p. 569). They believe that readers form a powerful connection with aesthetic words that are "deeply personal, familiar, meaningful and authentic . . . experienced for how they feel" (p. 569). Evocative writers accordingly draw on evocative language, or embodied prose, to convey felt sensations, images, and impressions.

Embodied writing evokes the sensations of life by painting a vibrant picture. Such details help us to inhabit the rich interior worlds of others as they stir up our imagination. Once these images materialise in our minds, we can play and experiment with them to construct new configurations of thought and feeling. To write in the *here and now* is to capture these formless sensations as "speak[ing] from the body . . . [is] a scholarship attuned to the visceral and somatic. . . . I am my body speaking. I am a mind/body fully engaged" (Pelias, 2016, p. 388). Through recognising the embodiment of our work, we may explore the ways knowledge is intuitively constructed, interpreted, and deconstructed and be able to shape it in new directions (Merleau-Ponty, 1967). Considering that intuitions are fleshed out at this nexus between the body and mind, I cast my net wide to catch what forms on the tip of my tongue. Tentative sensations become fleshed out as they are spoken or in the process of *becoming*. To put words to *barely-there* thoughts, I also read for what resonates in the *here and now*. This notion of writing in the present is explored further in the final chapter.

Embodiment, reflexivity, and social justice

Academics engage in embodied reflexivity when they explore how their bodies shape their perceptions. Burns (2003) introduces the term "embodied reflexivity" (p. 230) as a tool for identifying how the body impacts the production of knowledge, explaining how we assess the veracity of research accounts through our bodily sensations. Sharma, Reimer-Kirkham, and Cochrane (2009) define this "epistemology of embodiment," (p. 1643) through the following criteria:

(a) how researchers can be more aware of their emotions and bodily states,
(b) what these states can reveal about researchers and possibly their participants,
(c) how nonverbal communication is intersubjective and contributes to a co-construction of knowledge,
(d) how researchers' identities are multiple and complex, and
(e) how cultural difference can impact the interactions between researchers and participants.

Embodied writing reflects the varied nuances of our bodily experiences, indicating how our accounts represent one *truth* amongst many (Burns, 2003) as "we see aspects and profiles but never totalities" (Greene, 1995, p. 73). The ways we register our encounters differ as no one body or lived encounter is the same as another's. Embodied researchers acknowledge that although writing *about* and *from* the body is complex and messy; this complexity enables us to imagine the world in multitudinous and evocative ways (Sharma et al., 2009, p. 1648). Alternatively, by extracting the researcher's body from their inquiry, research can become contrived and one-dimensional, "obscur[ing] the complexities of knowledge production and yield[ing] deceptively tidy accounts of research" (Ellingson, 2006, p. 299). By writing about the body, we also permit those in physically marginalised spaces to express their affective and embodied knowing, and to speak authentically about their experiences. Academia becomes more equitable as spaces are generated for marginalised voices, "[as] embodied knowledges . . . not only render science more accessible to women and underprivileged communities, but also help cultivate citizenry for action and change" (Wilcox, 2009, p. 105). This leads Bhattacharya (2016) to assert that our "fragmented, similar, intersected, entangled" narratives, which touch on "marginalization based on gender, race, nationality, sexuality, religious affiliation, scholarly agenda, methodological preferences" (p. 310) help us to form connections with others and allow us to re-discover ourselves. Embodied writing cultivates greater authenticity as academic researchers can be *true* to their living body and shake off the pretences of "positionality, voice, labels, method, theory, ethics, and other crap like that" (Saldaña, 2014, p. 976).

Finally, embodied writers advocate for empathetic and compassionate understanding. Martin Buber depicts such complete and wholehearted understanding through a mutually reciprocating relationship, or an *I-You* form of knowing, in which the "I and You confront each other freely in a reciprocity that is not involved in or tainted by any causality; here man [sic] finds guaranteed the freedom of his being and of being" (1958, p. 89). The *I-You* signifies a mutual relationship, in which the *other* is not limited or controlled by the knower's constructions, and is deeply empathetic and imaginative, as the You stands, as "no thing among things, no event among events; it was present exclusively" (Buber, 1958, p. 89). Such deep empathetic connections form the richest and deepest form of human understanding. Embodied writing entails bringing words to life by allowing readers to imagine what the writer may be feeling in his or her body (Yoo, 2021a). We describe our embodied sensations so that others can inhabit them through experiencing their mood and feeling, thereby establishing readers as equal and reciprocal partners in the knowing relationship (Yoo, 2021a). The *I-You* consequently prevents us from drawing superficial lines that dehumanise and objectify; it brings us together instead through the mutual acknowledgment of our expansive humanity (Yoo, 2021a; Palmer, 1983).

Staying with the body

When we forget our embodied nature,
we mistakenly conceive knowledge,
as an analytical, pragmatic and objectivist enterprise.
This rigid view cannot account,
for the touches, tastes, sounds, sights, and smells,
that fix us in time and place.

Such thoughts emerge,
as I seek to express my embodied state.

. . . sitting on an open balcony of a sea-side cabin,
lost to the roar of distant waves,
enjoying the gentle breeze stroking my cheeks.
The constant movement,
the dull hum of my thoughts,
merging with the rhythms of the waves,
making me forget that I am separate.

The wider world pulses with an ebb and flow of energy,
dynamic and interconnected,
suggesting wholeness and belonging.
To know is to be at *one*.
There are no lines that separate.
There is no *I am*.

Activities for embodied writing

Exploring the inscribed *body*

1   What do you think people notice about you when they first meet you? Describe the physical features that initially draw another person's attention. What impact does their gaze have on you, and how does it shape how you perceive and relate to others? What effect do you think this has, if any, on the way you write? Write expressively about your thoughts.

2   The next time you are at a meeting, workshop, or conference, find a quiet space to sit and observe the people around you. Write about what or who you see. Note the small, but salient details of their body. Do they look engaged in their encounters? What makes you form this impression about them?

3   Take note of the bodily markers that represent age, gender, and ethnicity. Identify the bodily markers that have impacted how you engage and interpret the world. If you had been born into a different ethnicity or gender, or if you were at a different life stage, do you think your lens on life would differ? If so, how?

Investigating the lived *body*

4   Describe an encounter that you experienced on an embodied level. How did your body react to this encounter? What did your bodily reactions communicate to you? Write about this encounter in visceral terms through your sense of taste, touch, hearing, smell, and sight. Relate the bodily sensations that you experience as you recollect this encounter.

5   Topics of inquiry can emerge through our conversations, and often it is what a person does *not* say, rather than what they say, which speaks volumes. Describe the last interesting conversation that you had in your workplace. Recount the conversation through descriptions of your bodies. Reflect on what these bodily details may reveal about what was intuitively and implicitly felt.

Crafting words through the **lived** *body*

6   Take a section of the text and highlight the words, phrases, and language structure that resonate on an embodied level. Reflect on how the writer has crafted the lines or phrases to impact. Now write about the sensations of your body as you read this piece of writing. What do you think these sensations imply?

7   Practice describing your encounters as they are *lived* by your body. You may choose to draw on the excerpts of the previous writing activities. Move past conventional ways of constructing lines and sentences by breaking up lines with spaces, contrasting phrases, words, and metaphors. Repeat words and phrases to create a staccato rhythm or add commas to break up or stretch out your sentences to give the sense of an expansive, evolving space. Craft your writing with variations in sentence structure, paragraph lengths, and cadence to create a visceral effect of *felt* sense.

Reflecting on the body

8   How does the body influence how you write and what you choose to write about in your academic work? Does it have a central role or a peripheral one? Would you like to write about the body and in more embodied ways? Why or why not? If the body is not strongly featured in your academic writing, how can you adopt a more embodied writing style? Think about adapting a response to one of the exercises above into an academic paper that evokes the bodily senses.

3   Essence, resonance, and the expansivity of the poetic

Evocative forms of inquiry reveal the rich *essence* and the *resonance* that animates being and expression. Rather than focusing on superficial facts and information, they encompass deeper existential and ontological themes involving first concepts. As Sartre (1993) asserts, "understanding is not a quality coming to human reality from the outside; it is its characteristic way of existing" (p. 9). These ontological understandings are evoked through an artistic medium and experienced on a tacit and embodied level. Artistic forms are expansive enough to relay the essence captured by sensory and embodied knowledge, as Pallasmaa (2009) writes, artforms are "images of the hand and the body" that "exemplify essential existential knowledge . . . [such as] essence, inner structures and materials" (p. 19). Great works of art hence shed light onto the universality or timelessness of the human condition. They are also derived from the creator's lived experiences or "the identification of self with the experienced object, or the projection of the self on the object" (Pallasmaa, 2009, p. 132). Aesthetic and evocative inquiry modes encompass the richness and the mystery of presence, suggesting "an existential understanding and a synthesis of lived experience that fuses perception, memory and desire" (Pallasmaa, 2009, p. 116). The evocative accordingly illustrates how perception fuses with desire to convey the fullness of life.

Essence is felt and understood through rhythm. Rhythmic words move freely like moving water, with no other purpose but to maintain its flow. Ingold (2013) describes how tracing rhythm involves an "active following or going along" where the writer "mov[es] with forces and materials and follow[s] their lead" (pp. 2–3). Words flowing with essence retain an internal wavelength or rhythm that "educate[s] our attention, exercise[s] judgment" and moves in an itinerant or wayfaring fashion, or a way of learning-as-you-go . . . in often unexpected directions" (Vannini & Vannini, 2020, p. 867). Words flow spontaneously and, in all directions, as they contain an inner energy or intent that motivates, drives, and animates. This

DOI: 10.4324/9781003239987-3

itinerant flow of meaning unfolds dynamically within an emerging present. Graham (2020) explains how we *come into* our writing by engaging its rhythms, since ideas emerge when "the mind has been stilled by rhythmic, repetitive activity . . . hypnotised by the proverbial pocket watch swinging back and forth" so that it is the writer's task to tune into these rhythms and to be receptive to its "broadcasts" (p. 2). Rhythmic words flow so spontaneously that they appear to write themselves. Artists harness this natural momentum of affect and intent to craft creative works that equally inspire others (Pallasmaa, 2009).

Resonance *evokes* a mutual understanding of *essence* and emerges through an animating presence, life, or affect. Phalen (2015) asserts that resonance differentiates the aesthetic and intrinsically meaningful from the mechanical and superficial, as something deep within us activates when words carry essential or ontological meanings (p. 790). Resonance occurs on such an intrinsic level, passing along through rhythm, as "intensities that pass body to body (human and nonhuman), in those resonances that circulate about, between and sometimes stick to bodies and worlds" (Siegworth & Gregg, 2010, p. 1). These rhythms move one from one person to another, whether it be through bodily movement, sound, or words, "ris[ing] and fall[ing] not only along various rhythms and modalities of encounter" and "travers[ing] the ebbs and swells of intensities that pass between bodies" (Siegworth & Gregg, 2010, p. 2). This movement of affect or vibration occurs between bodies, which are in sync in a *unity of answerability* (Bakhtin, 1990; Phalen, 2015). Phalen (2015) experiences such answerability when he plays music with his friend Jordan and sways with their "chord progression." He loses awareness of anything beyond the song as he "let[s] the subdued rhythmical sound encompass and permeate [his] body" (p. 790). His unity with the energy or rhythm of the music is amplified by the resonance he feels between himself and his friend. Resonance manifests when these rhythms or vibrations harmonise, as Gershon (2020) states, "everything vibrates and oscillates . . . the vibrational affect of any single thing has the potential to resonate with any other possible thing" (pp. 1–2). To be receptive to resonance is to be answerable or accountable to others. In addition, when we allow vibrations to resound deeply within us, we become amplifiers of rhythm and resonance.

Life-imbued words are generative since resonance stirs life in others. Manheimer (1999) refers to Kierkegaard's notion of the "enabling dialectic" to describe writers who engage readers through "us[ing] language imaginatively to move the reader as they were moved" (p. 175). Resonance, or the feeling of mutual harmony, cultivates deeper and universal forms of understanding that can even bridge the barriers of a different language. As the anthropologist Wikan (1992) conveys, she could relate to the "Cairo poor" who "pour out their hearts" to her as they trusted that she would understand them (p. 472). She relates how we need to listen for resonance to "attend to what people say and the intent they are trying to convey, rather than groping for some larger answers within the particulars of their spoken words" (p. 467). Resonant listening allows Wikan to understand and empathise with the Cairo poor despite not having a shared language. Wikan (1992) equally encourages us to listen deeply and to be receptive to hidden *intent*, relating a conversation with a young Surati woman, who tells her, "It is very bad if you are sad and they laugh; that's why we hide our feelings" (p. 473). She illustrates how intent contains "what [is] at stake for people, the sources of their pain and humiliation" and asserts that we must listen *for* and *with* resonance to respect the intent embedded in words.

We can anticipate and imagine what is yet to come through resonance. It is a finely honed and receptive form of listening that catches what lies outside the range of everyday understanding. Resonant listening enhances our receptivity to reverberating sounds and vibrations, such as those that construct the melody of a song. Resonance allows us to pick up on the vibrations of flow and momentum so we can anticipate what will follow. It helps us to hum the next bars of a melody or tune or to swing our bodies to the beat of a song as we catch rhythm's spontaneous flow to cross the "border[s] between the not-yet and the yet-to-come and between dichotomies of virtual and actual, being and becoming, between 'life' and 'power,' and of recognition and representation" (Pearce, 2010, p. 903). Resonance moves beyond preconceptions and superficial constructions. It follows a vibrant and spontaneous path of discoveries rather than through rigid, formulaic, and predetermined steps. It embodies the richness of possibility.

Resonance helps us to determine veracity. Readers use resonating emotions and sensations to ascertain trustworthiness and to access latent meaning. We gravitate towards what resonates or appears familiar, finding comfort in what we have heard, seen, or felt before. The resonance we experience when we read allows us to "understand the text's claim on us: its concerns and concepts as they appear in this specific moment of reading" (Lind, 2020, p. 210). We question whether a writer's worldview resonates by asking ourselves whether we think and feel in similar ways. Reading for resonance involves crystallising, fleshing out, and actively filling in the gaps by referencing our own lived experiences. Resonance draws us in by activating and making visible our own unique sense making lens. This lens manifests when we become inquisitive about why something resonates and why we choose to tune into one frame over another. As we reflect on our interpretations, we can examine the multiple ways we can "put together, interfere, reinvent, co-create" new understanding (Lind, 2020, p. 12); as a result, we can become open to the possibility of alternative readings. Davies

(2017) explains this sense-making process through the analogy of a Shakespearian performance, describing how the audience "witness[es] the bringing to life of the material specificity of each character on the stage, the actors breathing life into the words on the page, inviting us into the emergent multiplicity and the flow of forces that animate them" (p. 268). Our writing resonates because we animate material words through inhabiting them with intent. As readers, we can also immerse ourselves in a writer's resonating intent to inhabit shared worlds.

Reading for resonance is not simply about attaining information but involves entering the rich experiences of others by *dwelling within* them. The greater the resonance, the more we can enter into shared meaning. Such resonant reading patterns emerge as I peruse academic papers. First, I catch the rhythm of the words as I read on a sensory and embodied level, not paying too much attention to the content, but letting the words wash over me. The vibrations of emotions and sensations take control as I "immers[e] [myself] in the flow of the story, lost in time and space" (Ellis, 2000, p. 273). Evocative prose is subsequently my primary tool for engagement. Ellis (2000) also describes how resonance guides her work as a reviewer. She relates how she "privilege[s] evocation over cognitive contemplation" and believes that if we can master the aesthetic and nuanced craft of evocative prose, we can manage all other kinds of writing (p. 274). Salvo (2020) reiterates the need to read for depth in the same way that we appreciate a painting to find its *truth*. Reading and writing accordingly becomes an embodied experience, as for meaning to be effortlessly grasped, the cognitive cannot interrupt (Ellis, 2000). Reading and writing evocative prose involves such receptivity and nuanced skill, since it draws on our capacity to intuit, imagine, and envision what lies beyond the surface.

Resonance acts as a barometer that signals when to speed up or slow down. My reading speeds up as I skip over parts that fail to engage and it slows down as words evoke pleasure and arouse my curiosity. Without resonance, my critical mind activates and reading becomes an exhausting and soulless chore. Ellis (2000) relays how a poorly written piece of prose "literally interrupts itself," as incongruences switch on the reader's "critical faculties." Such a story leaves the reader disconnected as it has "no narrative soul" and has not sufficiently "engaged, evoked, or provoked" (p. 274). When the critical mind is aroused, the magical spell that captivates and cultivates wonder is broken. As Pelias (2016) surmises, "the critical life produces a culture of broken bones" (p. 216), whereas evocative prose immerses you in an acoustical chamber that intensifies our curiosity and awareness of our rich social world (Ellis, 2000). Insight is evoked as aesthetically crafted writing triggers striking configurations of thought; new revelations can emerge when the critical mind is silenced.

Why the poetic?

> Each of us has a poetics of our life, a poetics of our physical life as well as
> our emotional and mental life.
>
> (Goodman, 2007, p. 147)

We draw on the poetic to depict the rawness of experience. The poetic can
capture essence due to its symbolic form. Goodman (2007) relates how
poetic writing captures the *poetic experience*, which sits at the intersection
of "human experience and soul . . . that which is unthinkable but capable
of feeling" (p. 143). A poet's subject matter revolves around the essence of
life, including "light, solitude, the natural world, love, time, creation itself"
(Sarton, 1985, p. 35). May (1994) similarly describes how artists can reveal
the underlying dynamics or the essence of a period through their intense
encounters. She relates how the creative encounter is determined by "the
degree of absorption, the degree of intensity . . . [and] a specific quality
of engagement," which conveys a sense of totality, coherence, and beauty
within the interlocking pattern of seemingly separate parts (p. 41). Poetry
is conceived as "the true work of the soul" as the poetic cannot be earned
or contrived because it is a gift that is given (Sarton, 1985, p. 28). The gift
of unfolding revelation appears so mysterious that it defies human understanding, transcending the "mind-body separation" and emerging from the
embodied, mysterious, and subliminal experience:

> Poetic writing is self-constructing and involves writing about experi-
> ence from a sensual perspective – centering, decoding, reframing, and
> discoursing literally as "embodied" participant observers, full of touch,
> smell, taste, hearing, and vision, open to the buzz and joy, the sweat and
> tears, the erotics and anxieties of daily life."
>
> (Lewis-Beck, Bryman, & Futing Liao, 2004, para. 5)

Words that convey the poetic experience are ontological rather than epistemological. Ontological knowing is not transactional or a means to an
end but forms a destination in itself. Not surprisingly, ontology refers to
metaphysics or the study of first or underlying principles about universal
matters; it delves into matters of essence (Dictionary.com, n.d.-f). Wikan
(1992) conveys the ontology of words as she seeks to depict the Balinese
life philosophy, values, and perspectives through her anthropology work.
She asserts that words should not contradict but should reveal what is
retained long after words are forgotten, describing how writing about the
Balinese requires finding rich words that capture their *essence*. The challenge of evocative inquiry is to craft such words that convey the raw inner

workings of life. Academic writers may turn to evocative forms as they find traditional modes too rigid and sterile to relay richness and complexity. Wikan (1992) emphasises the significance of affect in human understanding, arguing that "without feeling, we'll remain entangled by illusions" as we "reach for the sky with a short string" (p. 463). She believes that the descriptions of people should reflect a culture's inner character and being. To craft such writing is to convey *heart* or intent and to reach for the sky with the expansive strands of the poetic.

Language can be used socially in both an ontological and epistemological sense. Cunliffe (2002) explains how language can be employed as language-as-epistemology (as method) or language-as-ontology (as being). She conveys how the latter depicts the social world as being *constructed* through language, whilst the former suggests that meaning is fixed regardless of the social context. Language-as-epistemology is systematic and clinical in framing of knowing, whilst the poetic revolves around the principles of language-as-ontology, in which language is synonymous to *being* as it allows us to create our worlds and our identities (Lewis-Beck et al., 2004). To write poetically is to craft our realities through embodied action or *being in action* that conveys a sense of the present moment. Meaning emerges through responsive dialogue and unfolds in the *here* and *now* (Lewis-Beck et al., 2004). Three inherent precepts of language-as-ontology subsequently include creativity, the metaphorical, and the allusive (Cunliffe, 2002). Creativity refers to the social realities that are created as we read, speak, and write our way into meaning, whilst the allusive depicts the indirect meaning that emerges from imaginative expressions, such as narrative, imagery, and metaphors (Cunliffe, 2002).

Language-as-ontology highlights the rich, complex, living, and indeterminate nature of meaning-making. It emphasises the openness and expansivity of knowing, in which there are no fixed structures that govern how something should be understood or encountered. The ontological view further delves into the knower and receiver's interior worlds to encompass what goes beyond reported fact, reinforcing the social poetics' view that understanding is intersubjectively created between the knower and the known (Cunliffe, 2002). Poetic language heightens responsiveness by cultivating openness and metaphorical thinking, which allows individuals to become highly in tune and receptive to the *other*. Social poetics embodies this social constructionist perspective in which meaning, identities, and realities are shaped intersubjectively through daily interactions (Lewis-Beck et al., 2004).

Poetic writing triggers timeless, creative, and generative moments (Yoo, 2019c). In this expansive space, you can contemplate *what else*, in the way that "the engaging piece plays, opens closed doors, discovers hidden passageways, creates new spaces" (p. 376). Beauty transcends time's rapid passage to trigger deep insight though "creat[ing] an impression of something" within the flow of a passing moment (Cunliffe, 2002, p. 130). Such inherent creative potential is evident in the term 'poetic.' The word *poetic* derives from the Greek derivative *poiein* and refers to "images/imagining rather than literal meaning, about creating possibilities rather than describing actualities, and about multiplicity not specificity" (Cunliffe, 2002, p. 133). The poetic goes beyond the literal or actual and into the abstract; it rises beyond the sharp and rigid borders of specificity to encompass the nuanced and the universal.

The ethics of the poetic

Writing poetically helps me to navigate intense emotions and to find my feet when at sea. Hooks (2000) reminds us of its power by asserting that writing should "deepen the meaning of words . . . [so they] illuminate, transfix and transform" (pp. 1–2). Poetic words become a redemptive source of clarity that allows us to escape the academy's harsh pragmatism to engage the pleasurable and creative. It tentatively lights a way through the murky spaces of the unknown, and as such, each poetically crafted sentence reflects the uncertainty of an emerging thought. The poetic encounter embodies such *truth*-seeking by resembling the tentativeness of internal dialogue: as Sarton (1985) explains, "the poem is primarily a dialogue with the self and the novel a dialogue with others. . . . I suppose I have written novels to find out what I *thought* about something and poems to find out what I *felt* about something" (p. 29). Goodman (2007) asserts that the poetic reveals what lies in the gaps, writing, "That is what poets seek to make fluid and accessible, through the intuitive level of communication that lives in the gaps- the logical and emotive gaps- that poetic syntax provides" (p. 143). He identifies the poetic as being the language of the body because it embodies the fluid and undefined sensations of a lived experience, stating that poetry is written by the "body entire" to reflect the visceral, passionate, and bodily nature of human experience (p. 147). The poetic calls us to be "responsib[le] to develop ourselves, that is, to deepen ourselves within each moment, in each reality as it happens" (Goodman, 2007, p. 149). Whilst the poetic encompasses multiplicities, instrumental forms of writing cannot cater to paradoxes, ambiguities, or the richness of human life; it dulls understanding by limiting knowledge to what is measurable and quantifiable.

The poetic lens allows us to portray liminal encounters through beautiful and lyrical writing. Eisner (2006) argues that aestheticism must first be mastered to capture the poetic, since individuals can only depict the world as they perceive it. How we decipher the world may subsequently determine what becomes visible, since what we see may undergo a form of "imaginative transformation" depending on our level of sensitivity. Poetic writing cultivates a clarity and depth of sight by broadening what we can see and appreciate (Eisner, 2006). It facilitates the reflexive pauses required to reimagine new and vibrant possibilities:

> What poetry teaches us . . . is to create . . . gaps, silences, new forms of attention to live into, mapping moments that re-present the I-Story . . . the opportunity to be at cause- be the Artist/Writer of our experience . . . Poetry lends us the energy to respond and to write – in reaction. Energy-sharing-causing equal/opposite reaction.
>
> (Goodman, 2007, p. 150)

We experience the poetic by bringing words closer to their ontological or core meaning. To describe a timeless moment, poetic writers construct light, versatile, and expansive words that go beyond the literal. Their pace of words slows down to become contemplative, making the poetic a meditative experience. I once entered this poetic space when reflecting on the significance of breath. Through slowing down my breath and punctuating words with commas, my words could imitate the slow movements of an inhale and exhale, becoming "spoken-like and poetic; the silences, spaces, and gaps [being] intentional and eloquent, like a piece of music" (Yoo, 2019a, p. 400). Such writing feels *acoustical* because meaning stretches out and "the emotions retained in each word intensify" (Freeman & Rossignol, 2015, p. 389). Writing that moves as breath captures the deeper underlying emotions or the intent carried in our words. It exudes the vulnerability and authenticity of the simple and uncontrived acts of life.

To write poetically is to go out on a limb and to embrace the unknown. Poetic words are expansive enough to capture the fleetingness of emerging and tentative thought. They convey the hesitation, uncertainty, and exhilaration of vulnerability. Sarton (1985) reflects on the courage required to take the risks inherent to the poetic calling, as she relates how poets need to be "responsive and sensitive close to the surface, willing to give ourselves away. Such people rarely lead happy lives, but they do lead lives of constant growth and change" (p. 33). She believes that such an unprotected path is the only way to experience the full spectrum of life. Through a poetic lens, even difficult topics, such as violence, illness, and death, can be glimpsed through a softer light. A greater exposure to the pain of others may also make us aware of the subtlety, richness, and breadth of our human condition. Poetic writing can thus help us to tap into our common humanity to deepen our capacity for compassion and redemption; it may equip us with the eyes to see beauty in life's darkest moments.

How to create the poetic?

Openness and fluidity characterise the poetic. Poetic words resemble their subject; they are light and fluid enough to portray the tacit and expansive. Poetic writers draw on a repertoire of techniques and tools, such as metaphor, rhythm, salience, simplicity, indirectness, and ulteriority to craft a poetic moment. Striking metaphors and vivid configurations of language, for instance, can evoke intense feelings and insight, and the indirectness of the poetic form cultivates a contemplative mood required to dwell within words. The following section describes some features of the poetic craft, such as metaphor, rhythm, salience, simplicity, and texture.

Metaphor

Human beings can think metaphorically as unique symbol-using animals (Eisner, 1997). Metaphors convey the raw essence of experience by forming the symbols or images that represent our encounters, and these images and symbols can construct the canonical impressions that frame our perceptions (Eisner, 2006; Goodall, 2001). Such images become the memories that we draw on to make sense of the past, present, and future, since they are deeply imprinted through our sense of touch, taste, and smell (Altrichter, Posch, & Somekh, 1993; Clandinin & Connelly, 1988). Metaphors can generate new meanings and deeper insights by facilitating novel connections, revealing the insights that are often overlooked (Altrichter et al., 1993). We may say, for example, that time passes like water falling through open fingers to express our helplessness at time's flow. This metaphor highlights how it is as impossible to hold time or trap water as our fingers cannot remain still for long. Metaphors additionally generate new understandings by helping us place "dissimilar phenomena" side by side (Goodall, 2001, p. 11). Such a revelation emerged when I read Pallasmaa's *The Thinking Hand*, which describes the hand's central role in meaning-making. This metaphor took me by surprise because I had regarded the hand as a functional tool that carried out the mind's mandates. I had overlooked the hand's capacity to think and feel due to these narrow preconceptions. Pallasmaa (2009) introduces this idea, stating:

> The tool is an extension and specialization of the hand that alters the hand's natural powers and capacities. When an axe or a sheath knife is being used, the skilled user does not think of the hand and the tool as different and detached entities; the tool has grown to be a part of the hand, it has transformed into an entirely new specifies of organs, a tool-hand.

(pp. 47–48)

The hand was invisible even though it *touched* every moment of the day; it was simply an instrument that grasped tools and allowed me to complete life's essential tasks. My hands bore the marks of mechanical use, becoming lean and muscular from years of relentless movement. These instrumental uses masked other more intuitive and pleasurable movements, such as the sensations of tactile fingers lingering in cool flowing water or stroking my children's soft faces. By objectifying my hands, I had dismissed the richer understandings that lay at my fingertips and overlooked the infinitely pleasurable touches that bound me intimately to the world.

Metaphors also helped me to unlock what hovered in the liminal spaces of the *not yet*. I used the metaphor of *breath* in one paper to describe the life-giving and ineffable traits of poetic writing (Yoo, 2020c). Although I had noticed the core presence of *breath* in my work, it was difficult to express through words. I searched for suitable metaphors to explore this concept and came across *breath*. Breath appeared to be ever present, like the poetic potential within an encounter. Breath imbued words further contained the timbre of the writer's voice and resonated with lived experience. Like breath, metaphors seemed to reanimate essence and energy, embodying intent, as Goodall (2001) relates, "The relationship of symbolic interactions to material manifestations not just of words and actions but also of energy – or perhaps to see energy itself as an enabling metaphor" (p. 11). Through the metaphor of breath, I could recognise how writing's power came from the authority and animating spirit of the writer's inhales and exhales. This recognition encouraged me to seek words animated with presence and life.

Metaphors became a life craft that helped me to keep afloat. When stranded at sea with intense emotions, I searched for a metaphor to hold onto. For example, in Carolyn Ellis' (2011) *Jumping on and off the Runaway Train of Success*, the metaphor of a runaway train helped me to process my complex emotions about academia's chronic acceleration of time. The ceaseless stream of teaching, administrative work, and personal responsibilities had made me feel as if I had boarded a runaway train that was careering out of control. Feeling overwhelmed by the academic life, I questioned whether to continue down this hectic and out-of-control road or to jump off. Ellis (2011) expresses similar sentiments through the words of a junior colleague who questions, "How productive is it to live like this, with our work lives sucking the energy out of our personal and relational lives? What kind of toil does it take on our bodies and spirits . . . ?" (p. 160). Grams (2001) also uses the metaphor of a train journey to describe academia's rapid passage of time. Through his metaphor, I could explore my troubled emotions about academia's rapid pace. Grams (2001) describes the disorientating feeling of being on a train that flies past multiple stations, where all of a sudden, you find yourself winding down at the last stop, thinking, *where did all the time go*, as he relates:

You don't grow old gradually, or on purpose, the way you go down-
town on a subway. It's more like finding yourself standing in the last
station and wondering how you got there. For me, like the subway rider,
time has flown. Life was a busy business, marked by an almost frenetic
involvement with many things. I often felt, in the midst of doing something, that I should be doing something else.

(Grams, 2001, p. 100)

Metaphors bring to the surface the subconscious forces that shape and
drive. Richardson (2000) describes the negative impact of positivist academic writing discourses through the metaphor of being forced into right-
handedness by her father, despite being a left-handed person. She recollects
one memory of her father asking her kindergarten teacher to make her write
with her right hand, since he considers this to be the "right way" (p. 470).
After years of being compelled to use her right hand, the compulsion to do
so becomes so ingrained that drawing with her left hand makes her feel as if
she will be "chopped down." This leads her to draw "dark, decayed petals"
rather than a "full bloomed rose" with her left hand as her pleasure becomes
tainted and distorted (p. 470). Right-handedness is enforced until what is
natural feels unfamiliar, awkward, and illicit. She recollects:

Do you remember when I bought you left-handed scissors when you
were a kid and you didn't want them?" "They felt awkward in my hand
because I had learned to use the right-handed scissors in my left hand."
Metaphorically, maybe that's what I've learned to do.

(Richardson, 2000, p. 472)

Richardson (2000) uses this metaphor of being forced into right handedness to explore how mainstream academic discourses have curbed her natural creative writing voice. This metaphor allows her to reflect on a deeply
ingrained narrative that compels her to write in ways that do not feel unnat-
ural or pleasurable. Her metaphor resonated strongly as it reflected how
my academic writing training had equally negated my embodied ways of
writing. Richardson's (2000) metaphor shed insight into my circumstances
and gave me the courage to write in pleasurable and intrinsically meaningful ways.

Rhythm

Whenever we see, or more importantly hear language arranged in lines we
know we are entering the gallery of the poem.

(Lea, 2012, p. 68)

The poetic exists within rhythmic words. Rhythm can be found in artful arrangements of words and spaces that convey rich meaning. Awareness is heightened as each line break is composed to have the strongest aesthetic impact, as Lea (2012) writes how the poet is a "minimalist" who asks the question, "What am I trying to say? And, what is the best way to convey this thought or feeling?" (p. 70). She explains how words flow swiftly in prose, as opposed to the poetic form, in which words are "clarified, intensified and raised in stature. Words are experienced, not only as signifiers, but as objects themselves. At a reduced pace, meaning opens up and multiplies" (p. 68). Lea (2012) argues that a poet's skill rests in determining "where a line ends – or breaks," stating:

> Each line in a poem refracts into additional beginnings and endings inside the sentence, which grants not only heightened significance through emphasis – the start and end of a line are always hotspots – but lines also offer a sense of equivalence in which words and phrases can be weighed, or balanced, against other words and phrases.
>
> (p. 69)

Poetic meaning is suggestive and carries the pleasure of anticipation (Lea, 2012). Rhythm evokes anticipation and elicits engagement from readers. *Where will I be drawn to next?* Line breaks also follow the suggested movement of breath. Lea (2012) writes how Walt Whitman used breath to construct his poems, as each of his lines followed the length of a human breath. Rendle-Short's (2016) writing follows breath's movement as she uses commas to fragment lines and to reveal the rich hidden meaning held within in-between moments:

> Not "what happened there" in ICU, not "what actions played out," but the intangible, the unspoken, unbidden, the hard-to-conjure, the absence present in her body, presence left by her absence – the gaps between words and phrases in sentences, the held breath made by pause, the space between us marked by space (air and length). This scene is so emotionally charged.
>
> (p. 237)

The staccato form, conveyed through erratic line breaks, portrays the disjointed fragments and fractured sense of time. Rendle-Short (2016) highlights how syntax and grammar can be reinvented to craft meaning, commenting on how she crafts a fictional character who reflects on visiting her mother in hospital:

> If you can write a new sort of grammar on the page, this writer is asking herself (notice here in third person she is creating a new sort of

authoring self), if you can make the words do things you cannot do yourself – smell nearness of a body – perhaps there can be a different sort of grammar of relationship in the room of this hospital.

(p. 237)

Individual breaths reflect the movement of her thoughts. Intimacy is evoked by breaking conventional writing structures and forming uncommon parallels, such as, "smell[ing] the nearness of a body" to depict a world in which senses are heightened and "every triviality becomes imbued with significance" (Miller, 2012, pp. 237–242). Readers are brought into the breath patterns of the writer's body to occupy their spaces. By disrupting form and experimenting with syntax, punctuation, tense, vocabulary, and other grammatical and language features, readers can also shift familiar everyday conceptions (Cixous, 1998/2005). The novel heightens awareness, allowing significant details to emerge, as writing, "disrupts, [that] interrupts, [and] somehow opens up unforeseen ways of being, thinking, feeling, and knowing" (Bridges-Rhoads, Hughes, & Cleave, 2018, p. 817). Salience is further created by reconfiguring language and adopting "a new grammar," in which:

> We write sentences placing verbs by nouns, adverbs by pronouns, insert commas and full stops, choosing the order, deciding on cadence and rhythm, phrasing and syntax: tone and voice. To write is to noun, to verb, to sentence, to syntax. To write is to see, to ethic, as an infinitive marker.
>
> (Miller, 2012, p. 236)

Salience

Poetic time is slow and contemplative. Its leisurely pace allows us to linger and to see what was previously skimmed over. Sontag (1992) provides an analogy of *focused* gaze through taking a photograph, describing how a camera lens hones onto a particular frame to determine what the writer sees, as the writer "alter[s] and enlarge[s] our notions of what is worth looking at and what we have a right to observe" (p. 3). Sontag (1992) depicts this *honing in* on vision as a mechanism for recognising the profound. She portrays such concentrated forms of perception as an "ethics of seeing," as focused attention cultivates deeper levels of processing. Selective sight subsequently positions us in the world by determining what encounters are included or excluded from consciousness (Berger, 1977, p. 7). Our frames of reference register what *appears* prominent, so what one person actually *sees* or pays attention to may be different from another's. This allows certain encounters to become encoded as lasting memories whilst others simply fade away. Such snapshots open up a multitude of possible meanings, drawing attention to the knower's particular lens (Robertson & Hetherington, 2018). Tillett (2018) describes salience through a playful analogy of how a scanner can disrupt uniform representations of subject and time, as he relates:

> The effect of the image is that we perceive certain parts of the object increased in attention, while others are merely skipped over. We perceive a stretching of time, not just of image. We feel as if somehow part of perception itself has been captured: Where we spent increased attention yielded increased space in the image. Where we barely noticed is barely represented in the image. It is as if the common glances we take, varied in their attention and duration, are recorded creating a sort of visual representation of the varied flows of perception.
>
> (p. 2)

Our lens determines what is *seen*, and as we shift our lens, some things become hidden, whilst other details loom into view. Similar to a camera lens, a scanner can distort images to create a sense of "coming to attention after a day dream" as by altering the speed of its rollers, we can modify images to "undermin[e] our sense of time and perception, and, most radically, our sense of what constitutes an object" (Tillett, 2018, pp. 3–4). The metaphor of distorting images through a scanner illustrates how our subjectivities shape and colour our worlds. As evocative writers, we can equally vary our perceptions by reframing our lens, drawing out certain frames whilst passing over others. We can add colour and texture through poetic prose to offer up multiple interpretations of the world.

Simplicity, texture, and pleasure

Poetic writing is infinitely pleasurable as it allows us to *hear* our sentences in addition to *seeing* them (Colyar, 2016). The poetic does not overload the senses but allows us to inhabit a text in seemingly effortless ways. In *Writing into Position*, Pelias (2011) reveals how poetic writing provides a detailed description without overloading the reader. Writing poetically offers a "mouthful worthy of comment, encourages, lingering, savouring, remembering" (p. 666). Rinehart (1998) refers to Chekov's (1924) belief that good writers write with restraint, as grace is found in the "least possible number of movements" (p. 86). Simplicity is crafted through a "single well- thought phrase," cultivating a powerful sense of "being there" (Rinehart, 1998, p. 211). *Being there* is created through the careful blending of words. Nothing else but the *felt sense* lingers as we experience an encounter as it is *lived*, as Rinehart (1998) relays, "Writers need to experiment with point of view; sentence length and rhythm; dialogue (and tags); active and accurate vocabulary; and punctuation, nonstandard dialogue, and telling detail to make the story come alive" (p. 212). One must first be able to *hear* rhythms to craft it and to coax others into understanding. The poetic consequently seduces readers by allowing them to inhabit vivid and animated spaces (Colyar, 2016).

Texture can also add vibrant colour. Uneven surfaces, sharp and sweet tastes, and other varied sensations add richness and depth. Texture triggers multiple sensations that help us to form different associations and understandings. Multiplicities of meaning can equally arise from the indirectness and ulteriority of poetic writing. Figurative language "startles and enlivens" the mind as metaphors can be a comparison between dissimilar or contrasting things (Lea, 2012, p. 79). It carries the "connotation of one thing (the vehicle) to another thing (the tenor)," as the greater the texture, the richer the taste (Lea, 2012, p. 79). Differences in texture evoke the senses and varied dimensions that mirror the complexities and richness of human life: as Pallasmaa (2012) writes, "Elaborate surface textures and details, crafted for the hand, invite the sense of touch and create an atmosphere of intimacy and warmth" (p. 76). Miller (2012) depicts this richness found within multiplicities of meaning through *braided* words. She compares the taste of braided challah bread to ordinary bread and asserts that the latter has a far superior taste due to its beautiful form. She presents the moist and divine-tasting challah bread as a metaphor for the "inordinate pleasur[e]" of braided items, conveying how the *fragmentation* of poetic lines adds textures and layers, stating:

> This is what I love about all braided things: bread, hair, essays, rivers, our own circulatory systems pumping blood to our brains and our hearts. I love the fact of their separate parts intersecting, creating the illusion of wholeness, but with the oh-so-pleasurable texture of separation. It is not the same as a purely disjunctive form, the bits and pieces scattered like cookies on the baking sheet. Rather, the strands are separate, but together, creating a pattern that is lovely to the touch, makes the bread taste even better when we finally lift a slice of it to our tongues.
>
> (Miller, 2012, p. 243)

Artfully braided words can trigger fresh understandings. Cunliffe (2002) refers to such braiding of meaning as a form of "social poetics," in which a "living, responsive, constitutive process of meaning-making" process is evoked by the "indeterminate and self-contradictory" (p. 133). She reveals how the co-constructed nature of meaning generates infinite possibilities, stating, "As we struggle with the tensions and interplay of my voice/ your voice, my sense/your sense, what I am struck by what you are struck by, infinite possibilities emerge" (p. 130). This meaning-making process evolves indefinitely as we continue to construct new textures and braidings through our unique ways of feeling, thinking, and being. Braided or textured worlds trigger endless possible interpretations, and through resonance, we can intimately inhabit a myriad of multi-faceted encounters. Understanding deepens as we become receptive and sensitive to a widening pool of possible textures (Colyar, 2016).

Crafting words that feel

By focusing on the *felt* sense of words,
writing becomes poetic.
Poetic words encompass the poetic experience,
or the animating presence,
as Pallasmaa (2012) relates, "A great musician plays himself rather than the instrument,
and a skilful soccer player plays the entity of himself" (p. 71).

As I seek to write words that evoke life,
my prose becomes simple and fluid.
Lines become punctuated with commas,
to reflect the moving breath,
that gives life.
By experimenting with aesthetic forms,
my pleasure and enjoyment grows.

The poetic touches the subliminal,
through words that transcend the grind of everyday life,
to "re-mythicise,
re-sensualize,
and re-eroticize,
our relationship with the world,"
and to mediate,
"between the material and the spiritual" (Pallasmaa, 2012, p. 108).

To re-*mythicise* is to embody the fullness of our imaginative powers,
and to re-*sensualize* and re-*eroticize* is to revitalise with feeling,
to express *being* in the world,
and capture our thirst for life.

Writing activities to craft the poetic

Finding metaphors

1 Think of a metaphor that describes where you are in your academic journey. Spend the next few minutes unpacking this metaphor. Why did you choose it? What does it reveal about your academic writing career at this point in time?

2 Life may pass us by if we do not make time to contemplate, but such spaces are difficult to find with academia's accelerated pace. Think about how you approach the busy pace of academic life. How do you carve out the slow and expansive moments to craft poetic and evocative prose?

3 When you think of the word *poetic*, what images first come to mind? Does your current work reflect these words? If not, what are some ways you can align your teaching and research activities to the *poetic*?

Identifying the focus of your gaze

4 Go for a walk and take some photos of what catches your eye. What angles are these pictures taken from? What is pronounced? What is minimised, hidden, or obscured from view? Choose one of these photos and describe in detail what you can see. Write expressively about why you have chosen this view. What motivates you to focus your lens on this particular direction and angle?

5 Revisit a text you have written for an academic journal. Why do you think you focused on this theme, idea, or subject matter? Consider what makes it salient. What else could you have focused on or drawn out?

Exploring the poetic craft

6 Choose a metaphor that describes your writing style. Has this metaphor evolved over time? If so, you may see yourself entering new phases of writing that involves experimenting with alternative forms. Think about why these shifts have taken place. What were the main influences or events that have shaped the way you write now?

7 Listen to a piece of music that conveys a certain mood or feeling that you wish to capture in your writing. Follow its rhythm and try to replicate it through your words. Repeat this exercise with different types of music. Reflect on the following questions after completing the above

exercise. Which sounds help you to find flow in your writing? Why do you think this kind of music resonates with you? How are its rhythms mirrored in your words? You may need to revisit this passage, reading it aloud as you go, adding and deleting words and punctuation markers to create a raw and embodied atmosphere.

8 Think of a piece of art that resonates with your writing style. Describe the ways the artist used lines, colour, space to create mood and atmosphere. How does your eye move through the artwork? Why do you think it moves in this way?

9 To write poetically you may need to enter a poetic moment. Think of a pleasurable moment in the day, whether it was when you went for a walk, enjoyed a particular view, listened to a piece of music or savoured the first bite of a delicious meal. Describe these sensations in detail, choosing words and punctuation markers that echo how you savoured this moment.

Crafting the poetic

10 Reading a wide variety of poetic prose can help familiarise you with the craft of poetic writing. Find an academic paper that is poetically crafted and resonates with you. Identify a section that you would like to analyse. Use a highlighter to mark sentences that are phrased poetically to have an aesthetic impact. Reflect on how the writer plays with words and punctuation markers to create an aesthetic effect. Two examples of poetically crafted academic papers you may refer to are:

Gorman, G. (2018). This Girl is on Fire: Seeking a Home for the Narrative. *Qualitative Inquiry, 25(2)*, 163–165.

Rendle-Short, F. (2016). Parsing an ethics of seeing: Interrogating the grammar of a creative/critical practice. *New Writing: The International Journal for the Practice and Theory of Creative Writing, 13(2)*, 234–246.

11 Take a section of prose that you have written and restructure it using different line breaks. Read aloud the prose and the poetic version. Pay attention to how meaning has been condensed. Think about what has been lost and what has been gained in both versions (Lea, 2012, p. 72).

  Mark the spots where you have stopped for breath. Do these breath breaks feel natural? What do you think these line breaks suggest? What is highlighted or given prominence? Where else can you add commas or other language markers to slow down or speed up the pace of words? What impact do these changes in speed have?

12 Craft a poem. Take a piece of prose that you have written and transform it into a poem. You can use a response that you have composed for one

of the questions above, or a part of an academic paper you have written. Condense meaning by deleting any extra words. Add line breaks to have the maximum aesthetic impact. What emphasis is given as words become stripped down to their essence? Describe the mood or atmosphere of your poem. How does its impact differ from that of its prose form?

4 Crafting timelessness through aesthetic writing

Finding a timeless moment

When deeply immersed in poetic prose, time slows. Concentrated wholly on the act of reading or writing, we can step outside time's flow. Time no longer exists as you cannot see it passing. Heraclitus's "ever flowing river" has miraculously paused and we can still luxuriate in its refreshing coolness, despite not being able to "step twice because other waters flow by" (Mainemelis, 2002, p. 228). This chapter reflects on writing that frees us from the past or future by helping us to savour the pleasurable *now*. Such timeless moments can emerge when you are lost in the wonder and joy of reading and writing evocative texts. Alternatively, timelessness can elude when we mindlessly speed through our work, too busy moving on to pay close attention to the task at hand. When engaging in such instrumental forms of reading, we may become morally thoughtless by plundering the ideas of others to suit our purposes. When writing pragmatically, we may equally feel unfulfilled and alienated from ourselves. By reading and writing evocatively, however, we can slow the mindless flow of time by becoming fully receptive and attentive to the vibrant meanings of each word. I once wandered into such a space when contemplating the word *afternoon*:

> The word stirs up sensations of rest, winding down, saying farewell, and retreating from the outside world. The door has closed but not quite; there is that delightful anticipation of rest, the last lingering moments before the sunlight completely fades. Before being completely overtaken by darkness, there is time to pause and reflect. There is a sense of spaciousness, of expanding and suspended time.
>
> (Yoo, 2019b, p. 192)

The word 'afternoon' represented a lull in the day or a small pocket of bliss. It was a pause for a quick reassessment to let down one's burdens and

DOI: 10.4324/9781003239987-4

a magical moment imbued with feelings of rest. To write about the afternoon was to conjure the expansivity of darkness and to linger in the delight of anticipation. We slow down life's tempo by fleshing out the mysteries embedded in a word. The more we can flesh out their timeless meanings, the more we can dwell within a timeless encounter.

The ways we register time can reveal the richness of a lived moment, since time can run fast or slow depending on our level of joy and engagement (Csikszentmihalyi, 1990). Academics who write evocatively may find that time slows as they are immersed in what is creative and pleasurable. May (1994) provides a rationale for why this may occur, relaying how intense and direct encounters or deep absorption generates such a state of wonder and engagement. As such, an artist or scientist may become oblivious to the passage of time by being so fully immersed in a joyful activity, that they can experience the "emotion[s] that go with heightened consciousness, the experience of actualizing one's own potentialities" (p. 45). May (1994) expresses the power of the pleasurable and creative, stating that it can even transcend the physical limitations of death and decay. Not surprisingly, creativity and the arts are associated with the metaphorical pursuits of immortality represented by timeless works of art. This capacity for timelessness is encoded into the spiritual and non-physical element of our beings, or as the poet David Whyte (1994) writes, the eternal or timeless portion within us, stating:

> That understands physically what it means to live in eternity, where eternity is not an endless amount of time but an experience out of time, free from the stress of never being enough or having enough, a numinous experience of the present where we forget ourselves in the consummation of the moment.
>
> (p. 154)

Timelessness emerges when we lose track of time. It overtakes us when our senses are deeply engaged in an aesthetic moment. Manheimer (1999) relates how some encounters are so emotionally powerful that it seems as if there are "no befores and afters" (p. 164). This eternal and timeless *present* transcends all boundaries as attention is confined to the *now*. Pallasmaa (2009) describes how an aesthetic encounter deepens experience by slowing down or even suspending time, leaving a permanent impression rather than being a mere passing sensation (p. 17). He believes that canonical artworks attain their immortal status by "speak[ing] to us in the present tense" and transcending passing fads by dwelling on the immaterial and universal (p. 59). Timelessness manifests when we lose awareness of self as our focus remains fixed in the *here and now* (Mainemelis, 2002).

Moments become timeless as we lose our self-consciousness (Whyte, 1994) and become deeply immersed in a creative state of *flow*, which is characterised by a high level of engagement, intensity, and intrinsic motivation (Csikszentmihalyi, 1990). The experience itself becomes *the end* as understanding is fully embodied (Csikszentmihalyi, 1990). May (1994) further conveys how a heightened awareness does not mean increased self-consciousness, but an abandonment of the usual split between self and object; he uses the term *ecstasy*, which literally means to "stand out from" to describe this transcending of the normal psychological context delineated by the notion of time and the consciousness of the self. Here the state of ecstasy is neither irrational nor passive, but constitutes an integration of "intellectual, volitional, and emotional functions" (Mainemelis, 2002, p. 234). Ecstasy emerges as awareness becomes whole and is no longer split between the experiencing and the critically observing self.

Timeless moments are increasingly vital as the pace of living and scholarship speeds up. The desire for greater richness and meaning has led to the Slow ontology movement, which advocates taking the "time to do things properly" and to enjoy life (Honore, 2004, p. 208). Ulmer (2017) defines Slow ontology as time that has no boundaries or limits, since it encompasses diffracted and dispersed time and space in which matter moves according to different wavelengths and directions. She reflects on the timeless rhythms of slow ontology as "rooted in nature, it inspires more natural rhythms for our spatial, temporal, and material localities" thus offering rhythms that are different to ones that artificially segment and control our lives (p. 208). To move slowly is to be *present* to intrinsically meaningful, creative, and pleasurable work, and to reside outside the linear and instrumental rhythms that speed up time. Slow ontology embraces a non-linear time/space. Its rhythms transcend the moment by moving in all possible directions; it is diffractive and transcends notions of chronological or linear time, as Ulmer (2017) explains, "Slow Ontology is a diffraction – a dispersal – of time, space, and matter across different wavelengths, moving in different directions at different speeds" (p. 209). Time slows as we dwell on an expansive moment that is neither measurable, not linear nor chronological in movement.

The expansivity of timeless time

Poetic forms of writing embody timelessness and expansivity as they emerge during timeless moments (Yoo, 2020b). The poems embedded in this book equally unfolded as deep meditations on the chapter's themes.

Time would hold still during such moments because I was so fully engaged that I became oblivious to its presence. This desire to express timeless meaning through poetic prose is shared by other writers who craft exquisite prose when they lose an awareness of time. Lindquist's (2006) memoir *Rowing Without Oars* displays such timeless craftsmanship as she transcends the borders of her physical body to exist in a metaphysical space. Lindquist (2006) describes her body's rapid demise as she succumbs to ALS, conveying expansive meaning through each "well-thought phrase" to create a powerful sense of "being there" (Rinehart, 1998, p. 211). She expresses the preciousness of life by poetically depicting the loss of her body, one movement at a time. The simple and melodic rhythms of her words reveal how "emotionally sensed knowledges are the subtle knowledges, not knowledge of the emotions, but knowledge sensed through or by emotion" (Emerald & Carpenter, 2015, p. 741). She seeks to convey her experiences as she lives them, intensely and deeply. Her inner world flourishes as her outer world diminishes, and when she can only type with two fingers, each keyboard press carries the weight of her life.

Lindquist (2006) relays this point by describing an encounter with her son:

"Mummy, every second is a life," he says gently.

And he carries on: "You have hundreds of thousands of lives left, Mummy."

"Every second is a life," I echo.

(p. 87)

We can solve the problem of rapidly passing time by weaving timeless prose. By choosing simple words and through experimenting with syntax and grammar, we can convey an expansive sense of *becoming* (Yoo, 2020a). Without the energy to expend on any unnecessary movements, Lindquist's (2006) words are stripped down to bare essence. A feeling of continuity unfolds as her sense of 'I am' grows faint, as when we forget ourselves, the universal emerges. She meets this unknown presented by her weakening body head-on with "primordial strength. As when a child's head rotates out of the uterus" (p. 123). Her vision reaches beyond the physical realm and resounds like a bell that tolls from a timeless world, "I know that it will end. Make myself strong. Calm" (p. 123). It is this "primordial strength and calmness" that allows her to row her boat when she loses her oars. The oars represent an able body that anchors her to the world; they are the tools needed to carry out the tasks of living. Once she loses her grasp on these oars that tie her to the physical world, she can access a spiritual core that allows her to speak timeless words.

Lindquist (2006) lives a poetic existence through the *now*, as she writes:

> The whole of my adult life,
>   I have thought, it will be alright in the end. I have to do this first, then
> it will be alright.
>   But this way of thinking is no longer possible. The strange thing is
> that nowadays, when I am terminally ill, I feel moments of great joy,
> such as I have hardly ever felt before. Happiness has never been a con-
> stant for me, but now it is becoming one.

(p. 72)

Awareness of *essence* can emerge as physical life becomes increasingly restricted. Indeed, Lindquist (2006) develops a richer inner world as her body shuts down. She learns to filter out the unnecessary noise of life that distracts by recognising what holds intrinsic value, writing, "So many words are used to fill emptiness. Words are putty to fill cracks. To keep the darkness away and the lies alive" (p. 195). She reflects on how we keep ourselves busy as we fear the enormity of life, stating, "When we believe that everything has been said, the most important thing is left. The thing we defend ourselves against" (p. 195). Her illness teaches her to honour the preciousness of life, and to embrace her moments rather than squander them. An appreciation of essence further helps her confront her mortality, and in the final stages of her life, her writing becomes timeless poetry. Words retain the essence or intent as she writes as someone who is close to death, or in that liminal space between the physical and the spiritual, as she contemplates:

> The sea is choppy, with little white horses.
>   I settle myself comfortably on the deck and wait.
>   The wind rows me out, and I am at peace.
>   When it slackens at dusk I will have reached my haven.
>   Every second is a life.

(Lindquist, 2006, p. 196)

Timeless moments reside outside of time's flow. They are not historical, chronological, or linear as there is no beginning or end. Noriega (2006) contemplates this realm of timelessness, reflecting, "Lingering in the moment, each moment is stretched beyond its boundaries, until suddenly the moment itself falls out of historical time into some timeless realm" (p. 188). Lindquist's (2006) poetic and artistic forms of expression, which are awakened by the clarity of illness, reflect the timelessness of each moment. Her writing evokes a sense of wonder, revealing the potential for each moment to transcend space and time. Allan (2007) discusses this timelessness inherent to artistic forms, as he declares, "[the artists] bore triumphant witness to the power of beauty to accede to an eternal realm proof against the corrosive powers of time" (p. 4). Poetic writing contains an artistry that transforms prose into timeless artefacts. Pallasmaa (2009) emphasises this timeless power of the aesthetic, stating how historic works of art and architecture continue to touch as they allow us to "encounter the timeless present of a human being through the work, and consequently rediscover the actuality of our own being-in-the-world" (p. 132). Artworks appear timeless as they draw us into an expansive space, and we can equally experience a timeless self by becoming lost in their beauty (Yoo, 2019b).

Linear time

The expansivity and timelessness of the poetic contrasts against the rapidly ticking clock of academia. Linear time is driven by the instrumental and pragmatic lens of academia's critical enterprise; it denotes surveillance, boundaries, measurement, expectation, critique, outcomes. Pelias (2016) hints at the tediousness of critical or "performance-related" time that underpins academic work, as he describes the unrelenting mandate to *mark* and *judge* and relates how he "feel[s] the weight of the critical enterprise, the never-ending assessment" (p. 28). Pelias (2016) contemplates the value of a critical life, asking, "What does it mean to live with a critical eye, an eye that's always assessing, always deciding questions of worth, always saying what's good or bad?" (p. 220). He questions notions of value and legitimacy by asking what it means to say that "someone else does not measure up" and comments on how the critical enterprise can limit our freedom (p. 220). Carpenter equally questions the *critical eye* through describing the freedom of retirement, in which she can do what she pleases without any pressure of measurement or performance, as she writes, "One such freedom is the ability to read what I want to, when I want to and make comments without fear of real or anticipated recrimination or critique. I can document my story however I want to, without the constraints of style guides or the surveillance of directions to the author" (Emerald & Carpenter, 2014, p. 1146). Carpenter ponders the different choices she would have made had she had more time to reflect on her academic career path (Emerald & Carpenter, 2014). Her experiences illustrate how academic life can become constrained when it is measured by linear time. Linear time accelerates as it attempts to account for time by increasing productivity and performance, but to slow time, we must stand outside of time's flow to engage pleasurable and intrinsically meaningful work.

Our critical eye transforms time's flow into a chronological and linear process. In *Discovering the Spirit in the Rhythm of Time*, Grudzen and Oberle (2001) discuss two opposing perspectives on time. They refer to the Western view of chronological and linear time as *chronos* and to the Eastern view of time as *kairos*, meaning "outside of time . . . when time stands still . . . the mystical experience when time has meaning but no measurement" (p. 174). They describe how our industrialised and globalised world revolves around *chronos* time, since it is driven by economics and productivity and a *time is money* mindset, asserting, "Economic time productive time – is utilitarian and instrumental in its focus. In contrast, real leisure time is contemplative in its focus and does not attempt to possess or "manipulate the object of its contemplation" (pp. 177–178). Grudzen and Oberle (2001) explain how cyclical time is related to various forms of repetitive motion, which may be periodic (e.g., phasic, epochal, seasonal, etc.) or monotonic (i.e., subject to replication, recurrence, and prediction). The cyclic view of time is inspired by images of renewal, periodicity, and repetition, which is illustrated by the four seasons or the sunset cycle. The spiritual realm transcends notions of cyclic time by "transcend[ing] the bonds of measured time and explore the realm of timelessness" (Grudzen & Oberle, 2001, p. 171). This language of a spiritual or a timeless reality is captured by the aesthetic, as Pallasmaa (2016a) declares:

> Timelessness implies the encounter of idealised permanence, unaffected by the inherent fragility and temporality of life. The longing and quest for beauty is an unconscious attempt to eliminate the reality of vanishing time, erosion, ageing, decay, entropy and death. . . . Beauty is a promise; the experience of beauty evokes the presence of apparently permanent qualities and values – an illusion, no doubt, but mentally an important one.
>
> (p. 54)

To escape the harried life of an accelerated academia, I explore slower contemplative moments through pursuing creative and aesthetic writing that evokes pleasure (Yoo, 2019b). Writing creatively for its own sake is intensely pleasurable as the mind is free to play and is not objectified by the critical (Yoo, 2019b, 2019c). By weaving timeless prose, we may draw closer to solving the problem of limited and rapidly passing time.

Timelessness and grace

> The capacity to imagine, to liberate oneself from the limits of matter, place and time, must be regarded as the most human of all our qualities.
>
> (Pallasmaa, 2009, p. 17)

When our expression hits the mark, there is timelessness. Grace embodies this perfect resonance and the feeling of being whole or at one with oneself and the world. It manifests as effortless harmony, or an "elegance or beauty of form, manner, motion, or action" (Dictionary.com, n.d.-b). Grace appears outside of time's flow as it allows individuals to be so completely in tune with their surroundings that they appear to be driven by a source of higher intelligence. Grace also embodies *elegance*. There is an elegance to evocative writing as every word is beautifully positioned and aligned and minimal energy is expended to craft a message. Words flow naturally and in the most direct and *truest* path, resonating with Chekov's (1924) words, as "when a person expends the least amount of motion on one action, that is grace" (p. 97). There is no hidden agenda, nor any added complexities or unnecessary explanations. Meaning is expressed as it exists, made *so close* that you feel as if you *are there*. Words are unadorned, non-pretentious, vulnerable, transparent, and honest, materialising as if they are writing themselves. Little is withheld as prose comes about spontaneously and surprisingly like a gift that is freely given. Grace manifests in the effortless beauty of evocative writing that arouses endless pleasure and joy.

Grace suggests perfect unity and alignment. There is no sense of separation as words hit their target; both the reader and writer are unified and coexist as one through tacit, pleasurable, and embodied sense-making. Phalen (2015) describes such a form of merging and togetherness through a dialogical exchange between musicians, referring to Buber's (1958) ideas of a *living center* of a relationship, in which there is no inner and outer. There is only a sense of oneness and the timelessness within the living centre of an encounter. Phalen (2015) asserts that the centre of a musical encounter is found in a mutually reciprocal and shared present or the "sonic shroud" that forms as both the musician and audience "stand in relation to the living center of the song . . . [which] establish[es] a temporal and affective relation between self and other" (p. 790). He conveys how this embodied state elicits what Alfred Schutz (1971) defines as *durée*, or "the inner sense of time as expressed musically by the performer" (p. 790). Durée or internal time rhythms emerge as individuals become so engrossed in an encounter that they are unaffected by time's flow.

Durée materialised as I playfully explored rhythms that conveyed what was lived and felt (Yoo, 2019c). Becoming lost in these rhythms was to "linger in the moment, each moment is stretched beyond its boundaries, until suddenly the moment itself falls out of historical time into some timeless realm" (Noriega, 2006, p. 188). I also found that the tempo of my words could slow by becoming visceral, "roll[ing] off my tongue" with the lightness of the "gentle sunlight on my body and the tingling anticipation of words" (Yoo, 2019b, p. 152). Rigid structures of meaning broke down so that I could contemplate what else, in the way that "the engaging piece plays, opens closed doors, discovers hidden passageways, creates new spaces" (Pelias, 2011, p. 666). Such spontaneous, free, and uninhibited writing can allow us to see things in new and insightful ways, "creat[ing] an impression of something more when seen within the particular circumstance and flow of writing or conversation" (Cunliffe, 2002, p. 130). Evocative inquiry opens up these expansive spaces by providing endless opportunities for interpretation and exploration.

Evocative writing allows writers to connect with what is *lived* and *felt*. By writing evocatively, our words *flow* directly and spontaneously from a creative process (Elwood, Henriksen & Mishra, 2017). This flow or momentum signifies an entry into timelessness or an altered state of consciousness, where we become so immersed in an encounter that we lose awareness of self and time (Csikszentmihalyi, 1990). Ylijoki and Mäntylä (2003) refer to timeless time as "the experience of transcending time and one's self by becoming immersed in a captivating present-moment activity or event" (p. 548). Through writing evocatively, it is possible to find vibrant moments that exist outside of time's flow. As I reflect in one paper:

> As I write this paper, I am reminded of a high school teacher's English class on Ode on a Grecian Urn. The characters on this urn will never age as they are transfixed in time. They are engraved into this urn; time will never ravage their beauty. And even if the colour and lines of their bodies should fade, the yearning that they embody remains, forever recognised, felt and sensed.
>
> (Yoo, 2019c, p. 148)

Seeking timelessness

Each day I go through the motions,
surprised at how quickly,
days pass into nights,
weeks, months and years.
Where has all the time gone?
I ask, helpless at Heraclitus's "ever flowing river" (Mainemelis, 2002, p. 228).

Writing becomes a desperate attempt,
to transcend time's flow,
and to escape "growing sense of ontological insecurity" . . . (Ball, 2012,
    p. 20),
that passing time,
erases all that I do.

To account for precious time,
I mindlessly fill it,

with the tangible,
concrete,
and measurable.
But when time is quantified,
it accelerates.

Rather than measuring or quantifying,
I seek to slow down time's pace.
through evoking wonder and pleasure,
tracing rhythm and flow,
engagement so full,
awareness disappears.

Activities for crafting timeless prose

1 Tracking timelessness

Have you ever been so immersed in something that you lose track of time? The experience of timelessness often comes when you are completely absorbed in a pleasurable moment. Relate such a moment in your academic reading or writing experiences when time appeared to slow. What were you reading or writing about? How often do you experience such timeless moments in your work and why?

2 Finding flow

In a flow state we are completely absorbed in the *here and now*. Describe the activities that bring you into the present moment. Explain how you might capture some of these sensations of the *here and now* in your academic writing.

3 Writing for its own sake

Autotelic experiences occur when you engage in activity for its own sake. It is derived from the ancient Greek 'autós' meaning 'self' and 'télos' meaning 'result/outcome/end.' Do you consider academic writing to be an autotelic experience? Why or why not?

4 Exploring the new

Share a new experience that you have recently had. Such novel encounters can take you out of your comfort zone so that you may pay more attention to your context. Convey one such moment of venturing into the unknown or new. Write expressively about the sensations experienced in your body. What did you learn or discover about yourself?

5 *Temporal awareness*

Bringing awareness to the fleeting nature of experience can motivate us to savour the moment. Depict one moment when you were acutely aware of its fleetingness. What were you doing when this insight emerged? If you could take a picture of this moment and fix it in your memories, what would it look like? Recreate these images with as much detail as possible.

6 *Remembering a timeless moment*

Think about an aesthetic experience that made you lose track of time. It could be a moment when you were spell-bound by a captivating song or a work of art. What was your first reaction to this aesthetic experience? Why do you think you reacted in this way? Close your eyes and draw on your other senses to vividly depict this encounter.

5   Growth and generativity through narratives

Why growth and generativity?

Evocative writing *evokes*. It conjures up the colourful and vibrant by mirroring the richness of life. Rather than conforming to predetermined positivist and instrumental structures, it seeks to express the unknown through the aesthetic. *Evocative Qualitative Inquiry* traces this road to writing creatively and authentically in the academy. It asserts that academic inquiry must be first and foremost valuable to the self, posing Hendricks' (2008) question, "How do we integrate what we know with how we live?" (p. 113). Hendricks (2008) believes that by "turn[ing] the lantern light of inquiry onto one's self," we can regain authenticity and perspective; he therefore urges us not to offer explanations to others if they hold little relevance to ourselves (p. 113). Engaging in evocative inquiry is to turn the *lantern of inquiry* onto ourselves so that research accounts for the "messy packages lodged in life worlds that have been years in the making" (Hendricks, 2008, p. 113). The focus is placed on enriching both personal and professional worlds and so the value and impact of evocative forms of inquiry are enhanced. Richardson (2002b) reiterates the importance of research that deepens self-awareness, stating, "the research self is not separable from the lived self," since who we are and how we interpret our encounters is connected to our claims about legitimate knowledge systems (p. 887). As such, she urges us to write about our *lived* self despite the challenges.

We inquire evocatively to craft the sensations of our lived experiences and to not diminish the *other* (Eisner, 1991). Evocative words can have a strong impact by evoking vivid images that allow readers and writers to dwell within an encounter. These deep possibilities for knowing can lead to positive transformations and continual growth. This chapter explores the growth and generativity of evocative inquiry forms such as narratives. It parallels narratives to life to explore evocative writing's generative capacities. For example, a narrative and life both have textual and intertextual

DOI: 10.4324/9781003239987-5

components. A narrative is a text that progresses from a beginning, middle to an end, much like human life, which begins in birth and moves through specific developmental stages to culminate in death. The narrative form also follows a coherent pattern or a plot line, much like the snow-balling events that construct a life. The same vivid pattern making skills used to generate stories can accordingly be used to construct a colourful and vibrant life. Moreover, life stories and narratives can be read in multiple different ways to reveal their generative capacity, as both cater to endless ways of seeing and being. Life and narratives encompass such complexities and multiplicities that make them interesting and colourful, such as the intricate storylines, multifaceted characters, and ambiguous moments (Bochner, 2000; Bruner, 1990). The textuality and intertextuality of both mediums make them richly generative, as plotlines can evolve dynamically with each telling.

Writing a living text

Evocative forms of inquiry spark growth and generativity by stirring the imagination. Such generativity is inherent to sense-making or the text-making process, highlighting the fundamental "textuality – and intertextuality – of personal experience" (McKim & Randall, 2007, p. 149). In other words, we construct a *text* the moment we externalise our thoughts. We form a working picture simply by thinking or talking about our day, which allows us to process what we have yet to register on a conscious level (McKim & Randall, 2007). Narratives additionally present a chief means of translating *knowing* into an act of *telling* and for expressing the richness inherent to our thoughts. Life and narratives are complementary as life both anticipates and derives meaning from its telling (Bochner & Ellis, 2002). The act of telling involves recording the past, making sense of the present and forecasting the future. The narrative of an unfolding life represents this composition of a text or a *texistence* as we read and write out our life story in a continuous "back and forth" development of meaning (McKim & Randall, 2007, p. 149). Imagination allows us to form connections between isolated encounters to enable clearer and fuller interpretations of multiple possible outcomes (Chabot, 1985). By "reimagin[ing] the past," we can creatively craft the future as our memories construct the maps used to navigate life (Manheimer, 1999, p. 104). Storytelling sharpens our sense-making capacities or "narrative intelligence," allowing us to piece together events and construct a coherent plotline (Randall, 1999). Storytellers find patterns to move a plot line forward meaningfully as we "emplot, characterise, narrate, genre-ate and thematize," as opposed to moving in a random, haphazard fashion (Randall, 1999, p. 15). Randall explains that *emplotting* involves determining one's field of vision, as he writes:

To emplot: is to edit, editing is the essence of perception, via taste, touch, sight-seeing is to edit – i.e. by looking in one direction rather than another, focusing in one scene, it is to summarise, to find a pattern for, to fit the peculiar into the familiar, pattern seeking act, to relate the odd to the ordinary, to find an explanation for, identify possible sources, seek a resolution, meaning making act – to prioritise, what is more significant, censor the world so some things are weighed by consciousness, what is 'important' 'relevant,' to distinguish bet main and sub plot, to discern key moments/critical encounters and to place them in the story as nested event, an interrelated chain of events, to comprehend- construct them in narrative context as they 'unfold.'

(1999, p. 16)

The universality of storytelling reveals human beings as pattern makers who have a predisposition to organise their experiences into larger and more meaningful units (Bruner, 1990; Neill, 1994). Narratives provide meaning and purposefulness to human existence by placing isolated moments within "episodic units" (Polkinghorne, 1988, p. 36). This *narrative configuration* or the "drawing together [of] entities" reveal relationships between seemingly isolated aspects, which form the conceptual frameworks used to interpret the world (Polkinghorne, 1988, p. 36). Such an instinctive pattern forming trait, "go[es] back, way back, to the earliest of times, when men and women and children looked at one another, at the land, at the sky, at rivers and oceans, all mountains and deserts, at animals and plants, and wondered as it is in our nature to do" (Coles, 1989, p. 189). We construct a working picture by determining what becomes salient, and by questioning why certain events come about, as well as through finding resolutions to problems (Randall, 1999). Text-making involves tracing this flow between isolated encounters to form a "working picture (a moving picture, as in ever-revisable) of what we are like" (Randall, 1999, p. 17). As we explore and construct our frames of reference, we form a *provisional* understanding that undergoes further "text unfolding, lengthening, and deepening" (McKim & Randall, 2007, p. 149). This fundamental textuality of human life and narrative reflects our capacity to learn and grow.

Our narratives expand through this possibility for multiple interpretations, patterns, and plotlines. The connective and sequential patterns of a narrative's structure form a three-dimensional time/space that the storyteller navigates, moving between the past, present, future to reshape and reinterpret their encounters (Clandinin & Connelly, 2002). Van Manen (1997) introduces the term *logos* to describe writing that conveys meaning through its form. He asserts that a narrative's various plotlines reflect the openness of life, as both embody a similar expansiveness of possibility. The tentative and inconclusive nature of our writing reflects life's lack of finality as our plotlines are forever contingent on our changing circumstances. Ambiguities and the lack of finality further generate greater possibilities for interpretation, as Sparkes (1996) explains how we write narratives in a "disruptive, fragmented, and emotionally charged way . . . to resist an authoritative final interpretation . . . [or] [a] totalizing narrative structure" (p. 483). To make sense of this ambiguity, we pursue suggestive clues to anticipate events before they occur. Uncertainty and openness accordingly present opportunities to adapt and evolve our plot lines so that we can continue to flourish (Randall, 1999). Greene (2000) refers to such openness as the "consideration of the unfinished" and argues that growth resides within the activity triggered by a sense of incompleteness (p. 277).

We textualise our lives and author vibrant plot lines to derive agency and to "maneuver successfully through our day-to-day world" (Randall, 1999, p. 19). We *genre-rate* to *generate*, thematising and finding patterns amongst a random collection of gestures, comments, and events to derive meaning from our encounters. This pattern finding capacity underpins the storying process. It is what helps us align the past to the present, as well as to envision the future (Randall, 1999). Our agency or dexterity in constructing such plot lines deepens over time as we accumulate more life experiences and sub-plots. As Randall (1999) relates, "our life-plot thickens. Such thickening is an inevitable by-product of our immersion in time" (p. 20). He explains how this thickening or adding of layers allows experiences to become *sedimented*, allowing life to be a "continual[ly] de-composing, or composting" one's sense of self that enables a rich, moist, and depth of soil or range of understanding (p. 21). This capacity to build nuanced stories intensifies as we learn to approach life "sensitively and searchingly," so that it becomes an attribute or "an acquired talent, like the appreciation of great literature" (Randall, 1999, pp. 22–23). The emotional maturity and flexibility acquired over a lifetime can subsequently help us to craft richer and more vibrant texts.

Uncovering new plot lines

Our stories undergo the greatest changes through major disruptions, and the bigger the disruption, the greater the change may be. Significant disruptions can be transformative because we are forced to tap into an inner strength or deeper forms of imagination to envision possible solutions. Such experiences of adapting to change can also help us to become more flexible and versatile. Flexibility enables growth by allowing us to transcend superficial boundaries and limiting preconceptions. Rather than remaining fixed in our ways, we can continue to evolve by adapting to changing circumstances. Such expansive growth can eventually help us to draw closer to the universal. This leads Manheimer (1992) to surmise how individuals can reconstruct a richer self through overcoming conflict and by successfully navigating change and loss. Major life disruptions can shake us free from a mindless course so that we can consider contemplative alternatives, as Underhill (1999) concludes:

> To be spiritually alive means to be growing and changing; not to settle down among a series of systematized beliefs and duties, but to endure and go on enduring the strains, conflicts and difficulties incident to development.
>
> (p. 29)

Without change and growth, we stagnate. We become a lifeless shell that is driven by empty habits and routines, rather than an animating presence. Alternatively, a dynamic self is maintained through continual change as the self evolves to adjust to shifting circumstances (Manheimer, 1999). Adaptability to change entails inner growth and empowerment, as Manheimer (1999) declares, "how simple an idea, that by choosing it, I could change my personal history from a weight to a source of energy. Choosing was action, not reaction. So I said yes to my past, and chose it. And, almost at once, I felt a new energy course through my body and mind" (p. 50). The opposite of growth is the demise of our human faculties, as without the possibility of change and progression, our lives become stuck in a slow state of stasis or death.

Mainstream academic practices can inhibit flexibility and growth by trapping us in an endless cycle of achievement and productivity. Dominant neoliberalist academic discourses, for instance, position academic writers as consummate *producers* who need to maintain a steady stream of output. As inquiry becomes output focused and reduced to what is quantifiable, we forego the slower-paced creative and contemplative work. An output focused approach can additionally exacerbate anxiety, as no matter how much we achieve, it may never quite feel enough. Manheimer (1992) describes this approach as a form of *productive* aging, in which an individual's value declines as their productivity levels decrease. He asserts that the productive model is grounded in ceaseless activity, and that once all the activities come to an end, a sense of achievement and positive identity is lost. Major disruptions, such as illness or the loss of employment, can uproot this mindset by limiting our capacity to *produce*. By losing our capacity to engage in past activities, we may be forced to find other less output-driven ways to derive a positive sense of self.

Curiosity and openness can help us move beyond an output focused academic career. Curiosity motivates us to embrace challenges and to try out alternative paths despite our uncertainties. As Randall (1999) explains, "fear is what we feel when we tell ourselves that something terrible may happen in the future. Hope is, literally, a different story" (p. 21). Narratives of fear shut down, whilst those of hope and curiosity encourage us to embrace life's possibilities. Andrews (2012) reflects on the significance of this "forever becoming" reality of our human condition as she comments, "living through time, and in time, means something" (p. 390). *But what does this mean?* Perhaps it signifies that each moment carries a seed of possibility, which is to shift perceptions and alter our life's course, as Andrews (2012) declares, "the possibility for change remains within us till our dying day" (p. 390).

Expansivity and openness may intensify with age as the passing years free us from a sense of obligation. An awareness of limited time can motivate us to abandon task-orientated approaches to life, which may bring a sense of equanimity, as a "full acceptance of one's finitude leads to a sense of fulfillment and integrity or wholeness" (Manheimer, 2008, p. 95). Andrews (2012) glimpses this expansiveness in the human life cycle, as she observes her father playing with her four-month-old niece on his 85th birthday and reflects on how one generation contributes to the development of another (p. 392). She attempts to borrow his mature imaginative lens by asking his advice on how to live a meaningful life. Kotre (1984) defines this as a form of cultural generativity, in which the stories of older people convey a cultural or spiritual knowledge that enwraps their very being. Manheimer (2008) asserts that this generative self is not a "separate, private possession," but a "shared fabric of meaning that survives personal sorrows and joys and, as a contribution to the next generation, allows one to "outlive the self" (p. 95). Such generativity or *gerotranscendence* refers to the "shift . . . from a midlife materialistic and rational vision to a more cosmic and transcendent one, accompanied by an increase in life-satisfaction" and a withdrawal from every day, pragmatic, and materialistic activities to engage in more contemplative states (Tornstam, 1996, p. 38). Gerotranscendence allows us to move beyond the borders of multiple generations to draw closer to our universal essence (Tornstam, 1996). Writing evocatively is to equally continue transcending limiting borders and to reach a timeless core.

Growth and generativity through evocative inquiry

Evocative inquiry generates dialogue. Like a seed that falls to the ground to sprout a tree that bears its own seeds, evocative inquiry evokes new thought, feeling, and life. As Kotre (1995) remarks, "it's about the seed a plant has produced rather than the fate of the plant as it lies withering on the ground" (p. 34). These new seeds continue to produce more seeds so that the seed bearer's ideas can live on. The seed bearer's ideas thrive as they contain universal messages or core human issues that "remain ageless even in the face of great change" (Kaufman, 1986, as cited in de Medeiros, 2009, p. 98). People who engage in generative work or *self-realising* projects continue to pass down these universal conversations to others (Kotre, 1984). Their work is generative since they continue to evoke powerful responses and deep engagement from others. de Medeiros (2009) asserts that generativity facilitates a self-repair that counteracts the suffering caused by aging through "restor[ing] or repair[ing] a self in flux" (p. 101). She provides an analogy of an 85-year-old man who uses woodworking to explore his existential suffering, as the "unique, interactive and tangible entities" of his wooden artefacts "stave off threats to self and to create a sense of permanence . . . [of his] fading life" (p. 97). The man crafts his wooden artefacts and infuses them with a sense of self so that conversations about his work become generative and restorative. Moreover, the resonance that others feel towards his work allows him to derive a rich sense of *being* in the world. These ideas are captured by Pallasmaa (2009), who reiterates how the aesthetic invites "the viewer/user to touch the hand of the maker" by creating a powerful form of resonance that sets ourselves in a space and enables the "space [to] settle in [us]" (p. 104)

Growth and generativity are evoked through dialogue and interaction. Dialogue and interactions with others expose us to different worldviews, which allows our perceptions to widen. At its heart, evocative inquiry is about forming vibrant connections with oneself and others that enriches understanding. For example, evocative writers can facilitate deep knowing in readers by engaging them in a story (Bochner & Ellis, 2002; Ellis, 2004; Eisner, 1997). As readers listen to a story, they may also hear their hidden biases and the "vulnerabilities, conflicts, uncertainties, choices and values" inherent to their viewpoints (Bochner & Ellis, 2002, p. 748). Perceiving a story's 'truths' can enhance insightfulness and empowerment, as a well-written narrative deepens our imaginative faculties and our ability to perceive patterns of interrelatedness. As Eisner (1997) relates, "Narrative, when well crafted, is a spur to imagination, and through our imaginative participation in the worlds that we create, we have a platform for seeing what might be called our *actual worlds* more clearly" (p. 31). He suggests that stories enhance both the teller and listener's sensitivity to or empathy for the *other*, stating that a well-crafted narrative advances empathetic understanding as the listener actively looks for parallels between a story and their own lives to affirm their *truths*. Empathy and resonance facilitate this sense-making process so that readers can inhabit the encounters of others as if they were their own. Knowing feels complete because it is fully embodied.

Evocative stories steeped in vulnerability can create emotionally intense connections that derail everyday living. They can *evoke* by breaking open and healing a reader's heart (Bochner & Ellis, 2002). Strong emotional parallels between a story and a reader's experiences can drive such deep self-reflection. Coles (1989) relates how the powerful words of a gifted author, Tillie Olsen, triggered such a powerful 'pause' in his students so that they could reflect on their lives. His students can engage in the story's telling and fill in its gaps because it resonates with their own lived experiences. Reading becomes this magical dialogue between a listener's own understanding of a story and a story's revelation of itself. Evocatively written narratives may additionally spur powerful action by breaking open and moving the readers' hearts. Coles (1989) quotes a favourite English professor to explain how a story becomes significant by triggering positive changes in action, stating, "there are many interpretations to a good story, and it isn't a question of which one is right and wrong but of what you do with what you read" (p. 47). These changes in action demonstrate how understanding is not static but continually evolving.

Narrative understanding offers up alternative viewpoints that activate new lines of inquiry (Clandinin & Connelly, 2002). Each reader reinterprets a narrative from their unique perspectives, weaving in insights so that the story continues to evoke growth and life. Nye (1997) explains how rewriting past narratives in a positive and redemptive light helps us to fight against future adversities. Coles (1989) relates an example of a patient who confronts his illness using fiction, describing how the fictional account allowed his patient to safely access what had previously evoked terror. Furthermore, displaying past hurts and wrongs can break individuals free from vicious cycles of guilt and pain by helping them take responsibility for their past (Frank, 1995, p. 132). Stories of illness consequently become a form of witnessing to the conditions that strip others of their voice as storytellers engage in an "ethic of solidarity and commitment" by using their own stories of suffering to heal others (Frank, 1995, p. 132).

Generativity and artistic vision

Changes in the plot line move a story along. Positive changes can occur even in the most challenging circumstances to reveal the power of redemption. This redemptive potential is acutely visible in end-of-life narratives, which mark the period when physical vitality begins to diminish and fade. Restrictions to the physical world through aging and illness highlight how a rich inner life can transcend bodily limitations. Banerjee, Wohlmann, and Dahm (2017) illustrate this notion through the examples of two famous artists, Monet and Baryshnikov, who deepen their aesthetic craft despite their increasing frailty. As his eyesight diminishes, Monet transforms the individual textures of his brush strokes into homogenised structures to convey "detached contemplation" that "transcends outer appearance" (Arnheim,

1978, pp. 152–153). These thicker blended strokes allow his paintings to embody a greater expansivity and depth. Baryshnikov, the famous ballet dancer, also transcends his aging body by giving a powerful performance with a heart monitor (Banerjee et al., 2017). The monitor becomes the centre-piece of his performance, breaking preconceived notions that the aging body does not dance. Both artists illustrate how a diminishing body could create an opportunity to reconstruct and re-imagine oneself to enhance his artistic vision (Banerjee et al., 2017). They demonstrate how losses can become a generative force that embodies renewal, versatility, nuance and depth through our imagination and resilient spirit. As Andrews (2012) relates, "while our physical ability to hear certain sounds declines as we get older, our ability to listen increases; the physical process of ageing may be accompanied by a rethinking of the use of our senses" (p. 390). Rich meaning hence resides in the redemptive capacity to transcend limitations rather than within a productive and able body, since an "artist's aesthetic power, his or her genius of artistic expression" does not reside in physical prowess, but in re-envisioning outer limits to enhance their inner life (Banerjee et al., 2017, p. 10). Challenging circumstances can deepen our creative vision by forcing us to re-envision ourselves, and this artistically enhanced vision further reframes possibility.

Generativity is possible regardless of life stage. Retirees may experience rich opportunities for growth as their professional obligations come to an end. Growth is possible as they reimagine their identities through a more intrinsically meaningful and less pragmatic lens. Manheimer (2008) uses the metaphor of a "vortex of nothingness" to describe the desolation that awaits some retirees who may feel "all that [they] have done and been is now useless to [them]" (p. 93). He asserts that even the most significant professional achievements will fade away, stating, "the nothingness of retirement can seem like a death in life, leaving what remains a protracted postmortem existence" (p. 93). Manheimer (2008), however, emphasises life's redemptive possibilities by depicting this vortex of nothingness as a rite of passage into a more mature and expansive state. He believes that although a safe passageway is not always guaranteed, we need to pass through this fiery vortex to attain "authenticity and wholeness, if not immortality" (p. 97). He compares this journey to the Jungian exploration of the unconscious, in which we encounter "archetypal images of a collective nature" to build a more emancipatory, resilient, and timeless self (p. 95).

Generativity as a calling

We are born to tell stories, as by telling and retelling stories, we can better understand our experiences (Bochner & Ellis, 2002). Evocative forms of writing, such as personal narratives, are one form of *moral* work as they help individuals to, "live a meaningful, useful and ethical life" (Bochner & Ellis, 2002, p. 747). The listener takes on an active role through the story-teller's skill of evoking compassion, as they become "morally, emotionally, aesthetically, and intellectually" engaged (Bochner & Ellis, 2002, p. 745). They can further spur on the generative process by listening actively as Charon (2005) relates how, "this imaginative, active, receptive, aesthetic experience of donating the self toward the meaning-making of the other is a dramatic, daring, transformative move" (p. 39). She asserts that listening is fundamental to healing, as listeners can validate a teller's words through attentively "absorbing oceanically that which the other says, connotes, displays, performs, and means" (p. 39). Medical practitioners demonstrate such ethical listening by attending to a patient's ailments through the unfolding story of their life, rather than a diagnosis, respectfully acknowledging that "story, yours, mine – it's' what we all carry with us on this trip we take, and we owe it to each other to respect our stories and learn from them" (Coles, 1989, p. 30). Listening ethically contrasts against the "moral thoughtlessness" of medical practitioners who value answers over the person as they are solely focused on fixing or diagnosing their patient (Coles, 1989, p. 18).

We listen respectfully to bear witness to an unfolding story. Generativity lies at the heart of respectful listening as it embodies an openness to growth without pre-empting or closing off with premature conclusions. The analogy of the seed, which falls to the ground to become a tree that bears more seeds, epitomises this generative nature of evocative inquiry. Vibrant meaning continues to evolve by triggering powerful responses from others; and by engaging others through creating rich evocative accounts, we become agents for growth. Through inhabiting the shared spaces of an unfolding story, we can empower others to shape incomplete and limiting storylines into more life-evoking ones. Evocative inquiry becomes a profoundly moral act as it cultivates deeper, empathetic, and respectful forms of understanding. This innate capacity for rich growth and generativity is poetically described by Bruner (1990) as the "art hidden in the human soul" (p. 15). We express the artistry of our soul by crafting meaningful and convincing life stories that rejuvenate and regenerate. Each moment or action retains this poetic possibility for growth and generativity, as Rilke (2004) describes:

> A hand lying on the shoulder or thigh of another body no longer belongs completely to the one it came from: A new thing arises out of it and the object it touches or grasps, a thing that has no name and belongs to no one, and it is this new thing, which has its own definite boundaries, that matters from that point on.

(p. 44)

Activities for constructing generative prose

1. Savouring a moment

Spend a few minutes free writing about a pleasurable moment. As you write, describe in detail the various sensations that felt pleasurable, expressing your ideas as they materialise. Spend a couple of minutes reflecting on the feelings that arose whilst constructing this text once you have finished. Share your writing with a friend. Ask them about which words and phrases resonated most with them and what mood they caught from your words.

2. Cultivating a generative state of mind

There are many opportunities to find new topics to write about in everyday life. The next time you take a walk or speak to a colleague, slow down and empty your mind of your preoccupations. What do you notice as you tune into the present moment? Write expressively about this encounter. Revisit your writing after a few days and highlight the details that you have tuned into. Why do you think these details have stood out to you?

3. Generative conversations

Talk to a colleague about their research. Ask them how they approach the academic writing process. Next, ask about what kinds of academic research and writing they would like to do if they did not have to worry about research outputs. Is it the same as the academic writing they are currently doing? If so, ask them how they came upon this path of doing the work that gives them joy.

4. Generating alternative perspectives

One way of generating new thoughts is to try and dwell in the shoes of another person. Draw four quadrants on a piece of paper. Write the following words in the quadrants: seeing, doing, thinking, feeling. Next, consider an encounter that you had with someone where you expressed a strong conflict in views.

In each quadrant, write down the relevant aspects of each perspective. For example, you may write about what you saw during the situation, what actions you noticed in yourself and the other person, what you were thinking about as the encounter was taking place and what emotions you were feeling. Now, turn the page over and create another quadrant using the same headings. Fill out the spaces from the perspective of the person who did not see eye to eye with you. Write expressively about your experience of completing the activity. What insights emerged as you tried to see this encounter from the other person's perspective?

You can extend this exercise by crafting a richly embodied account of this encounter from the other person's perspective. Include as much detail as possible about this person's bodily movements, facial expressions, and speech to convey how this person may have felt.

5. Metaphors and divergent thinking

We can apply a similar generative perspective to our academic writing. Think about a paper that you have been working on. Have you used a metaphor or image to enter into your writing? If so, which one? Brainstorm other possible metaphors that you could have used instead. How would your argument change depending on which metaphor you chose? Which metaphor aligns most closely to the message you want to convey?

6. Generative creations

All creative acts speak *of* and *about* their creator. Think about a piece of music, an image, or a text that you created that resonates with you. Share it with someone else. Ask your friend or colleague about what impact this work had on them, i.e., how it made them feel and the insights that emerged.

7. Collecting artefacts

Think about a paper you have written that inspired a creative response from another. What aspect of your paper resonated with them and triggered their creative response? Alternatively, think of a paper that evoked a creative response from you. Describe what aspects of the paper inspired you to craft your aesthetic response.

8. Asking generative questions

Generativity revolves around our capacity to ask and to pursue our questions. Write down the questions that emerge through your reading and writing. Record these questions in a journal. Write expressively about why these questions resonate with you. See what thoughts emerge.

Often an important question can emerge from the thoughts that preoccupy your mind. Where does your mind wander off to during the day? Why do you think your mind keeps returning to these thoughts? Follow this trail of generative questioning to uncover your deepest concerns.

6   Hearing voice

Why *voice*?

After many years of faltering through the academic writing process, I had given up hope of finding *voice*. I abandoned writing forms that gave me pleasure and focused on conforming to mainstream academic writing conventions to increase my publication record. But by rejecting my embodied ways of writing, I eventually became alienated from myself. Without an authentic voice, my words seemed to contain no heart, standing empty like an old, abandoned house, with no sign of its occupants. To write with voice, however, made me feel as if I was crafting a message that could endure due to its colourful and warm presence. These experiences gave me insight into how an expert craftsman can imbue their spirit into their craftsmanship, filling it with an animating presence that could *move*. Pallasmaa (2009) writes about expertly crafted work that speaks of "dedication, determination and hope," as he describes, "the unity of a shoemaker's professional world and his (sic) hands, the dark workshop of a blacksmith covered by soot and the smell of burning coal . . . the fully integrated atmosphere of a cabinet-maker's persona" (p. 50). He acknowledges how individuals have made a pact to make one's trade the ultimate destiny of life, training his or her hands for the highly specialised tasks of making their craft their life's work. Pallasmaa (2009) asserts that a craftsman's creations mirror his or her spirit, stating:

> The painter's hand does not only reproduce the visual appearance of the object, person or event- observed, remembered or imagined- the hand perfects the impossible tasks of recreating the object's very essence, its sense of life, in all its sensory and sensual manifestations . . . . In addition to breathing life into the scene, a profound work projects the object's metaphysical essence, and in fact, it creates a world.
>
> (p. 85)

DOI: 10.4324/9781003239987-6

Voice eventually emerged as my academic and personal worlds converged, as the more personal my writing became, the more I could hear my *voice* speaking through it. The tone of my words felt light and warm, contrasting the cold starkness of the omniscient voice of scientific rationalism. Even when hearing someone speak, I was drawn towards the sound of their voice rather than any of their logical arguments, as Carnegie and Esenwein (1915/2017) assert, "A rich, correctly-used voice is the greatest physical factor of persuasiveness and power, often over-topping the effects of reason" (p. 100). Writing evocatively about lived experiences led to this recognition of *voice*, as the more the voice spoke, the more I was compelled to listen to it. Writing evocatively was ultimately about naming my reality so that the world could become more vibrant and less hazy. Words became compelling acts of authorship, speaking loudly and powerfully about who I was and how I perceived the world. Richardson (2001) describes writing as a way of *being*, relating how it allowed her to piece herself together after a major car accident by re-constituting her sense of self in the world. Her words had resonated as I too regarded writing as a way of constructing a *life*.

Evocative inquiry evokes authenticity, authorship, and presence. Pallasmaa (2009) relays how the creator's work is imbued with his or her affective and embodied self, which lives on through the creator's imagination. He argues that there is no higher source of authority than *voice* and asserts that shallow and weak artists require constant external validation, whilst those who possess authority speak from their own embodied knowledge. To evoke is to affirm one's own voice and to prevent others from speaking for us (Goodall, 2001; Pelias, 2005). It is to express our own understandings, rather than filtering them through the "perspectives, agendas, interactions, and interpretations" of others (Lapadat, 2017, p. 593). Murray (1991) equally proposes that all writing is autobiographical as our encounters are interpreted through our subjectivities, whilst Colyar (2009) declares that we name our reality through our writing as we manifest how we make sense of the world. Writing accordingly becomes "the act of say-ing I" (Didion, 1976, p. 270). Evocative writing facilitates self-affirmation as we can distinguish our own thoughts and feelings from those of others by speaking from the personal (Badley, 2016; Witherall & Noddings, 1991). Uncovering our voice is to adopt greater responsibility for our feelings, thoughts, and actions, and to embrace a "commitment to speak the truth" about our circumstances (Frank, 2016, p. 21). Such an internally consistent discourse makes evocative writing an act of emancipation and empowerment.

Voice becomes visible through being heard (Bakhtin, 1981). We come to *know* a voice by hearing it speak rather than by contriving it. There is no formula for acquiring voice as it unfolds rather than being fabricated. Academic writers listen to their voice as they follow their vocation, which Murray (1986) conveys, posing the question "We are lucky to have a vocation of scholarship, a calling. But who is calling? Ourselves . . . write for yourself – try to figure out what you want to say rather than what other people want" (p. 147). *Voice* constitutes the realisation of this higher calling to take responsibility for one's own life. Manheimer (1999) refers to Stanley Cavell's (1994) explanation that "authorship, a public act, is always an act of authority, a self-proclaimed right to speak for oneself that makes a story out of unformed experiences and events" (p. 176). We actualise our calling as evocative writers by pursuing our innermost desires. As Moi (2017) writes, "The text [is] a kind of action, whereby intention becomes something which is embedded in the text rather than something exterior to it" (p. 202). Intent also becomes visible through words that are masterfully crafted, as "every masterful exercise of craft projects determined intentionality and an imagined vision of the completed task or object at hand" (Pallasmaa, 2009, p. 52). This notion is equally expressed by Carnegie and Esenwein (1915/2017) who comment, "if the thought beneath your words is warm, fresh, spontaneous, a part of yourself, your utterance will have breath and life" (p. 67). In this way, an artist's vision is brought into being, so that "art creates images and emotions that are as true as the actual encounters of life" (Pallasmaa, 2009, p. 132).

Words are made powerful by our whole-hearted intent, which embodies authority and authenticity. Nikolić (2016) compares this intense "relationship between the depth of meaning and the intensity of sensation" (pp. 4–5) to the power of being completely engrossed in a work of art. Wholeheartedness and a unified intent penetrates and implies total absorption, "mov[ing] in oneness with the object, where one's awareness completely unifies with its point of reference" (Goleman & Tarcher, 1977, p. 71). *Voice* or words animated with affect constitute the perfect pitch. There is no *object*, but a *subject* that is moving and pulsating. Vibrant words *move* as they encompass the emotions that "pulsat[e] with vigor and energy;" this notion is captured through the Latin stem 'vibrans,' which means "to shake, move to and fro" (Dictionary.com, n.d.-e). Movement suggests life, momentum, and energy, as without movement, there is no *subject* that gives an encounter meaning and life. Words that do not move are dull, lifeless, and static; they become an empty shell or a catatonic body, frozen in time and unable to evolve. The term 'catatonic' has consequently been associated with "muscular rigidity and mental stupor" or being in a "daze or stupor; unresponsive" (Dictionary.com, n.d.-d). To be catatonic is to be incapacitated in body, mind, and feeling. Catatonic writing reflects this rigid, unresponsive, and *voice*-less state. Words give no hint of the author's presence; as a result, they fail to inspire or animate. There is no presence with which to form a connection or relationship; there is no dialogue that can evolve. Dewsbury (2014) warns how objectivist and instrumental forms can deaden thought, feeling and expression, forming "a gravestone" for our thoughts (p. 150). He highlights how the opposite of words animated with *voice* are those that become a tomb for empty thoughts.

Academic writing that is without voice is static, inert, and lifeless. It does not carry the life or breath that animates and moves. When holding onto breath, for example, my words appear linear, transactional, and overly purposeful. There is no space for spontaneity or creative expression. Such writing flows rapidly without reflection or thoughtful pause, constricting rather than expanding and causing anxiety to overflow. Alternatively, to write with breath or voice is to challenge lifeless and regimented approaches and to playfully craft prose that reflects a rich engagement with life. Life imbued words can energise, like how breath activates every cell in our bodies. Breath-inspired words enliven and transcend, "orient[ing] the reader reflectively to that region of lived experience where the phenomenon dwells in recognizable form" (van Manen, 2002, p. 238). Words animated with presence and voice further suggest the continuation of life, change, and the potential for regeneration. Voice accordingly deepens and enriches through exposure to a myriad of life experiences. In their descriptions of an artisan's craft, Vannini and Vannini (2020) describe how *aliveness* is a process of *becoming* that reflects our "capacity for growth" (p. 868). They assert that materials are living and do not simply exist as objects for our interpretation, but act as subjects that possess "the force to inspire change, generate growth, and redirect our learning journeys" (p. 5). Materials can subsequently come alive as they are animated with the creator's or artisan's presence.

The significance of voice in academic writing is further reflected through our actual speaking voice. If you were to hear me reading these sentences aloud you would be able to hear a *soft* and tentative voice . . . *sounding* out words *slowly* . . . mirroring the process of unfolding through a one-step forward and two-step sidewards rhythm. Sentences inch forward slowly with the hopeful anticipation of discovery. There is also a growing firmness in tone and intent as words gain momentum. Colapinto (2015) equally stumbles upon the significance of the spoken voice as he suffers an injury to his vocal cords that transforms his voice into a cudgel rather than a scalpel. He can no longer express his dynamic self as his voice can only convey "a more monotone, less enthusiastic, less engaged personality" (para. 30). His vastly transformed voice expresses a small sliver of his dynamic personality, revealing very little about the person who occupies his body. This experience teaches him how our unique vocal acoustics express our vitality and communicates volumes about our emotions, personality, and professionalism. He explains how prosody conveys our emotional state of happiness, anger, or excitement, and embeds intent into our words so that we can "woo, persuade, threaten, cajole and mollify" and describes how the word prosody derived from the ancient Greek word *pros*, meaning 'toward,' and 'ody,' meaning 'song' (para. 26). Colapinto (2015) concludes that we "speak toward song" rather than through monotone so that our voices express affect, as well as how we define ourselves (para. 26). Ellis (2009) equally touches on the richness of song-like speech as she describes how she feels drawn to "melodious voices" (p. 373).

In addition to prosody, there is cadence, which refers to the rhythmic flow of words or sounds and the modulation of tones (Dictionary.com, n.d.-c). Cadence is conceived as the vital stream of emotions underlying our words. Carnegie and Esenwein (1915/2017) write how it is these inflections or lilts in our voice or the "little upward and downward shadings of the voice" that are most revealing (p. 56). The fact that we modulate our tone and speak towards song suggests that voice intimates what is song-like, that is, the essence or poetic core that drives a poetic existence. Our voice hints at who we are by expressing what lies within the depth of our beings. Colapinto (2015) relays Aristotle's view that voice is produced by the soul, which can manifest in "high, clear sustained note that an opera tenor hits" that creates shivers up our spine (para. 37). He conceives voice to be a mystery as it conveys intimate and poetic details of a person through "tiny ripples of air that we beam into other people's brains" (para. 31).

Becoming receptive to *voice*

Academic papers that resonate appear to be speaking directly to me. They contain a warm and intimate presence that offers me companionship and light up the path ahead. Many such writers helped me to forge a path towards expressing voice. When I read *It's about Time: Narrative and the Divided Self* by Arthur Bochner (1997), I was beginning to heal the rift between the academic and personal. Bochner 's (1997) epiphany about academic writing that harmonises both worlds struck me like a bolt of lightning, revealing vibrant and intrinsically meaningful possibilities for academic writing. I could feel Richardson's (1997) strong presence through *Fields of Play: Constructing an academic life*. Her courage helped me to navigate the tenuous path of writing from my personal voice, despite my fears of rejection from my academic peers. Sparkes' (1996) *The Fatal Flaw: A Narrative of the Fragile Body-Self* motivated me to write my first autoethnographic paper about my body. Sparkes' (1996) vulnerable depiction of his recurring back injury helped me to share an equally embodied experience that overhauled how I existed in the world. To develop my evocative writing craft, I read journals such as *Qualitative Inquiry, New Writing: The International Journal for the Practice and Theory of Creative writing, Cultural Studies* ←> *Critical Methodologies* and *The Qualitative Report* to glimpse ways of crafting creative and vibrant words that resonated. An autoethnographic conference workshop on the writing of Helene Cixous was also a key turning point. Cixous's (1993) *Three Steps on the Ladder of Writing* introduced me to the spirit of words that captured the essence of life. Her description of the School of the Dead motivated me to write with abandonment and to grasp the vitality awakened at death's door. I consumed these vibrant texts that spanned across diverse academic fields to glean their insights about human life. These eclectic voices spoke with the authority of lived experience to revitalise my understanding of academic writing.

The legacy of voice

The true significance of voice was unveiled when I saw it as a gift of presence that continued to live on. The idea of voice as *legacy* emerged as I listened to a colleague talk about her next writing project. Although we had both enjoyed reading and writing creatively, she had not yet explored creative forms of academic inquiry despite authoring several academic books and countless journal articles. With retirement looming on the horizon, she desired to write about something closer to the heart. What would be a *worthy enough* project? We pondered this question in silence when she suddenly mentioned her desire to write a book that her children could remember her by. Her words took me by surprise. Who thinks about *death* as their next writing project? I revisited these thoughts later, considering what the gift of presence could mean for her loved ones. Her words could be a legacy for them to remember her, carrying a vitality that could bring her back to life. I wrote *Tracing the Immaterial Spaces of You* in light of our conversation, as a meditation on living words that became a continued dialogue with one's loved ones (Yoo, 2021c). This paper was an exploration of immortal words that capture a writer's non-perishable essence.

These words resonate with Cixous' (1993) descriptions of the School of the Dead, in which individuals become a "guardian, the friend, the regenerator of the dead" by learning to write words that retain their living presence (p. 12). The School of the Dead teaches us to capture the vitality that can only be accessed at death's door. To write in the *light of death* is to create something "vivid. Colourful, striking, and with an abundance of feeling" (Yoo, 2021c, p. 66). Death reminds us to write vibrantly and whole-heartedly as there is no coming back from it: as Cixous (1993) relays, "writing is learning to die. It's learning not to be afraid . . . [it] is to live at the extremity of life, which is what the dead, death, give us" (p. 10). Such writers lose themselves to their work and forsake all sense of a tomorrow; they are the salt of life, as they unearth the rawness that frightens and makes us "tremble, redden, bleed" (Cixous, 1993, p. 32). Cixous (1993) believes that this *truth* is acquired at the end of one's life, as we become honest when we relinquish "all the lies that have helped us live" (pp. 36–37). Such lies keep us in a state of mindlessness by telling us to pursue external measures of achievement as this is *what matters*. The end of life, however, shatters the falsities as we realise that time is finite and cannot be wasted (Cixous, 1993). To be mortally wounded is to be gifted with this clarity of sight that uncovers *truth*. The School of the Dead accordingly teaches us to write with presence and to craft words that contain "permanent traces of you, the parts that feel so real and near, the ones that would speak in your place" (Yoo, 2021c, p. 68). Words become gifts as you animate them with your presence and "infus[e] them with breath, mist-like; they carry something esoteric that transcends the material world" (Yoo, 2021c, p. 68). These words appear timeless as they continue to live on. To write with *voice* is to speak words that bring your intimate presence to life. Alternatively, to write without presence and voice is to "snuff out life" by objectifying yourself and your readers (Yoo, 2021c, p. 68).

The writer that speaks

We write to disclose something unpublished; we make our thoughts visible to make sense of incomplete storylines and to direct new possible paths (Van Manen, 1997). Writing with *voice* provides such an opportunity for "insightful praxis" so that we can become more thoughtful perceivers and authors of life (Van Manen, 1997, p. 130). Perceiving writing as a craft is to choose how we will express ourselves (Van Manen, 1997). For this reason, writing has been described as a form of portrait-making as it reveals the writer's unique sensemaking lens. A portrait highlights what the artist sees and his or her particular style of crafting a picture, which leads Lawrence-Lightfoot and Davis (1997) to describe research portraits or portrayals as self-portraits that reveal the researcher's *soul*. Our painting becomes a manifestation of what we see or what looms into focus. Evocative forms cultivate such a deeper understanding of self, and through aesthetic forms of expression, we can encounter the world and "our own being-in-the-world in an intensified manner" to develop a richer understanding of self (Pallasmaa, 2009, p. 132).

To conclude, I bring the focus back to the *what*, to answer the *why* and the *how* to sharpen the focus of inquiry. As Manheimer (1999) relates, "I had started out by asking about *what* something might be. . . . As the conversation evolved, I found myself shifting from *what* to *how* – wondering *how* it might be to know" (p. 295). Moving from the *what* to the *how* suggests greater levels of contemplation, reflexivity, and critical insight, since it involves shifting our focus from what we see to how we frame our perceptions. By glimpsing the tacit and unconscious forces that shape our perceptions or voice, we can reimagine alternative ways of perceiving and being. This chapter contemplates this *how* by exploring voice as a writer's animating intent or breath. Expressing voice allows us to craft words that resonate with presence. *Life*-infused words create a sense of personhood so that readers feel as if they are conversing with the writer, such as within the intimate spaces of a letter. Thoughtfully composed words, which are spoken directly from their maker, continue to *live on* in the minds of others.

Writing exercises to cultivate voice

1 The stranger in the mirror

At the beginning of my academic career, I would read over my academic papers and be unable to get a sense of the author. When this happened, I felt as if I was looking in the mirror and not recognising my own face. Through writing evocatively, this face became clearer, more intimate, and expressive. The more I wrote, the better I could sense the voice that animated my words. When we read words and cannot get a sense of our voice, we may become a person who looks into the mirror and cannot recognise his or her own face. When you read your writing and reflect on its tone, what image comes to mind? If you were to depict your writing voice as a portrait, how would you describe its features? Are these features sharp and clear or are they blurry? What style of writing makes this picture clearer or fuzzier?

2 Alignment between the professional and personal

Often the faces that we see in the mirror differ depending on the type of writing we do. The 'face' that manifests in our academic work, for example, may be different from the one that appears when we write for pleasure. Do you write outside of academic work for enjoyment? If so, how does the writing style or voice or your non-academic writing differ or align with your academic writing? What kinds of faces do you see reflected through the different types of writing you do? Which of these feel the most like the *real* you?

3 The voice that evolves

The face that we see can also change over time. The face that was reflected at me at the beginning of my academic career was so fuzzy that it appeared to belong to an anonymous stranger. None of her features appeared familiar. The lines of this person's face became more definite as I wrote evocatively, until there was greater detail, depth, and dimension. When I was reading over my writing one day, I could finally see a warm pair of eyes gazing back at me. Have you experienced something similar? Has your writing style evolved throughout your academic career? If so, how? What have been the pivotal encounters that have shaped it?

4 Voice portraits

Some academic writers can compose their words in ways that make you feel as if they are sitting and speaking directly with you. Their voices are so intimate that you are almost able to visualise their faces in your mind's eye as you read their work. What kind of voices resonate with you? To get a sense of tone, it is useful to reflect on the writing of your favourite academic writers. Pick three different academic writers whose work resonates. Note the ways that they craft their words, sentence structures, and punctuation to communicate a certain mood and atmosphere. How would you describe the voice of these writers? Why do you gravitate to their work? If you were to create a portrait of their voices, how would you depict their features?

5 A metaphor for voice

Using a metaphor to describe the sound and feel of your voice can trigger new insights by allowing us to form connections with the familiar. Choose a metaphor that describes your voice as an academic writer. Spend a few moments describing why you have chosen this metaphor. What does it reveal?

6 Experimenting with voice

In the earlier chapters, you experimented with punctuation, sentence structure, and vocabulary to construct a particular mood. Refer to your written piece on a metaphor that reflects your academic writing voice. Alter the punctuation, sentence structure, and language so that the prose resonates with the metaphor you have chosen. How does the voice of your text change as you experiment with different words and language structures? Which of these 'voices' feel authentic or resonate with you?

7 The sound of voice

How does your actual voice sound when you speak aloud? Is it husky, high or low-pitched, clear, modulated, grainy, lyric, or slow or fast paced? Relay its pitch, timbre, pace, and volume etc. Does your speaking voice reflect the voice that emerges through your written words? If so, how? If not, what are the differences and what do you think they imply?

8　*Developing a vibrant voice*

Find a passage from one of your academic papers and read it aloud. What mood does it capture? What emotions and thoughts does it convey? Now change the punctuation and the choice and configuration of words so that your sentences flow more vibrantly and energetically. Compare the original text with the altered one. Which resonates better with you and why? Read these texts aloud so that you can compare how each *sound.*

9　*The voice you project to others*

Often feedback from your peers will give you some idea about your unique writing voice. Recently, a colleague signed off one email to me with the statement "whatever you write will be filled with your distinctive voice of empathy, sensitivity, and insight" (J. Manuel, personal communication, March 30, 2021). Her words gave me insight into how others might perceive my *voice.* Think about the passing comments people have made that reveal the distinctive traits of your writing voice. What terms have they used to describe your writing style?

10　*False or inauthentic voices*

Early in my career, I wrote densely theoretical prose to increase my chances of publication. Academic writers who are setting out on their careers may equally feel compelled to adopt a certain writing style to be accepted by their peers. Reflect on the writing style or voice that you project through your academic papers. Do the words feel familiar and flow smoothly? If not, think about what strategies you could explore to let your voice speak.

Another question you may ask yourself is whether you write primarily for others or for yourself. If you find that you are more motivated by attaining a publication rather than writing for pleasure, you may find that your writing style may be more influenced by the expectations of others.

11　*Letting voice speak*

Letter writing is an activity in which you converse with another person. It revolves around a relationship of intimacy and shared understanding. Even the first word . . . *Dear* . . . is one of endearment and places an immediate focus on the recipient of the letter and your relationship with him or her.

Through letters we can show our care and share our lives with another person. Our authentic voice accordingly emerges naturally within the intimate spaces of a letter. If you find it difficult to find voice in your academic writing, try crafting your words in the form of a letter. This letter can be directed at yourself or to an academic peer whom you admire for the evocative writing style. Try writing a thank you letter to someone in the academic community for a paper that he or she had written that resonates deeply with you. Describe the aspects of their paper that resonate and explain how it has enriched your understanding of academic writing.

7   Faith and evocative inquiry

Why faith?

Crafting aesthetic and vibrant words that evoke is *hard, hard, hard.* Many exhausting evenings are spent tapping away to the soft glow of a laptop to craft feeling and tone. There is the tedium of endless rewriting and the possibility of a crushing rejection, which can feel like a rejection of self as you write vulnerably about your life. The evocative inquiry path is uncertain and may not lead to external measures of success. What holds you firm is the belief that the unknown holds immeasurable beauty and worth. Pye (1995) expresses these sentiments through a definition of two types of workmanship, which he defines as the "workmanship of risk" and "workmanship of certainty" (p. 9). He argues that risk-orientated workmanship carries the possibility that the creator may "ruin the job" through "inattention, or inexperience, or accident," whilst the latter leads to a certain outcome as "the quality of the result is predetermined and beyond the control of the operative" (p. 9). Pallasmaa (2009) appraises the workmanship of risk as being far superior, declaring, "All the works of men [sic] which have been most admired since the beginning of our history have been made by the workmanship at risk" (p. 72). Risk-orientated workmanship embodies an openness to what is possible; its core premise is that without risk, we cannot reach the heights of expression, knowing, and being. Evocative inquirers demonstrate this *workmanship of risk* as they write vulnerably and courageously, treading a tenuous path to uncover what has yet to be disclosed. They believe that manifesting what is *not yet* requires a receptivity to the tacit and non-concrete. Dewsbury (2014) expresses this mysteriousness of knowing by acknowledging how silences can often convey more than words themselves by embodying the expansivity of the ineffable. The aesthetic can capture this ineffable by encompassing what is sensed, rather than what is registered by our consciousness, having "an impact on our mind before it becomes intuited, or without ever being intellectually understood" (Pallasmaa, 2009, p. 127).

DOI: 10.4324/9781003239987-7

A paradigm shift occurred when I began to write to inquire about the bigger life questions, such as why we are here, why we do what we do and who we think we are. These questions can emerge as we experience the rich complexities of life. Gorman (2018) reveals how life's mysteries can only be deciphered after deepening one's understanding through "decades of stumbling" through and navigating life's trials (p. 165). She understands how these experiences have enriched her understanding so that she can now write to honour her stories and to inhabit their mysteries. Gorman's (2018) experiences reveal how writing can *atone* as it captures the magical vibrance of our experiences (p. 165). Such a realisation leads Goodall (2004) to declare that research involves "work[ing] out the mysterious," as words are "magical symbols; constructions capable of establishing relationships, communities, and empires; and yet also full of the fairy dust capable of altering, changing, or dissolving" (p. 6). Evocative writers affirm this inherent mystery of inquiry as they regard it to be "a subtle and nuanced thing. Born of the spirit, it lives in between the empirical world and an ethereal one, connecting that which appears to be the individual case with accounts that rely on interconnected and holistic underlying causes" (Goodall, 2004, p. 8). Evocative writing can connect everyday lived moments to these fundamental and universal *truths*, revealing the vibrant flow of energy or magic underpinning life.

To write evocatively is to capture the tacit and ineffable. Pallasmaa (2016b) depicts this mysterious unfolding of meaning through the aesthetic craft of architecture, asserting that architects craft harmony in their work, "similar to [the] musical tuning" that accounts for the "diffuse and peripheral perception in motion" and the "omnidirectional, multisensory, embodied." He contrasts this to the "focused perception and the static gaze" that separates the onlooker as an outsider (p. 129). Evocative writers equally tune their musical receptivity by harnessing underlying rhythms of affect and intent rather than focusing on superficial and concrete facts. Pallasmaa (2016b) relays how rationalist and positivist thought cannot grasp something as nuanced as mood, stating:

> Mood seeps into our mental constitution in an unnoticed and unstructured manner, in the same way that we feel temperature, humidity or the smell of the air, unintentionally and in an embodied manner. Altogether, mood is closer to an embodied haptic sensation than to an external visual percept.
>
> (pp. 129–130)

Artistic and evocative prose invokes resonance, mood, and atmosphere. Pallasmaa (2016b) relates how architects craft and heighten mood through their designs to "evoke specific tunings and desires," similar to how a novelist or a theatre director can "articulate and sustain specific moods in order to create the dramatic flow and continuum of the narrative" (p. 130). He describes how *mood* is instantly and vicariously communicated omnidirectionally through smells, sensations, and feelings as it encompasses the overall feeling, ambience, or atmosphere (p. 130). Pallasmaa (2016b) concludes that the expansiveness of the "fragmented and discontinuous mosaic" can capture what is complex and mysterious, rather than the "automatic, objective and precise" (p. 133). The evocative and aesthetic is one such expansive medium that caters to ambiguity and multiplicity and conveys nuanced meaning.

Having faith means openness to the mystery

> What might happen if we linger longer at those sites where we might otherwise collapse into our habitual processes and understandings? What new thoughts can be forged and how? What sense can be made?
>
> (Pearce, 2010, p. 903)

To see and feel the magic of the unknown, you must first believe it exists; moreover, by paying attention to the possibilities of the *not yet*, we can bring it into being (Goodall, 2008). This liminal and anticipatory space between *what is* and *not yet* is "an intermediate, highly particular state akin to a sort of suspension between ignorance and enlightenment, which marks the end of unknowing and the beginning of knowing" (Lugli, 1986, p. 123). Undefined and in-between spaces present a fertile ground for discovery, resonating with possibility and hope (Pearce, 2010). By bridging the gap between our desired realities and actualities, we can invoke "imagination, envisioning, creating, and desire" (Pearce, 2010, p. 902). Hope emerges from these in-between spaces that exude the possibility for the *what else*. Hope manifests in the anticipation of a rich life and the expectation of continuous learning. It is found in everyday spaces, such as a passing comment, facial expression, or gesture, which can animate new thoughts (Maclure, 2013). These details stir the imagination by revealing the possibilities of multiple perspectives and various interpretations, creating a trail of anticipatory meaning. Such an outlook can be likened to the refracted lens of crystal that disperses light in multiple directions.

An open mindset allows us to see beyond the limitations of our preconceptions. Coles (1989), a medical practitioner, reflects this state of openness through listening to patients' stories with less "conceptual static" to form a more accurate understanding of their illness (p. 19). He relates how we need to perceive what is *present*, rather than automatically deferring to our preconceived formulas or mental conceptualisations. Coles (1989) refers to these conceptualisations through the Greek root 'theamai,' which relates to "something visual in our minds" (p. 20). The word *theory* thus signifies an "enlargement of (our) observation," rather than a "complex [form of] theorizing" (p. 20). To *behold* is to see beyond the limiting frames of preconceptions, premature conclusions, superficial settlements, or partial truths, which are formed in the rush to find an answer. Openness prevents us from seeking easy answers or opting for one extreme over another to achieve a superficial consensus (Miller & Stroh, 1994). It further discourages us from resolving dilemmas by choosing one option at the expense of another, preventing what is ignored from festering in the dark (Miller & Stroh, 1994). Openness to complexity, ambiguity and paradox generates growth, as individuals immerse themselves in opposing forces to form new and creative connections (Miller & Stroh, 1994). This dynamic power of coexisting opposites is visible in the potential of the *not yet* or in the creative act, in which something is generated from nothing. A painter embodies the possibility of the *not yet* by seeing all possibilities in *nothing* to create a marvellous painting from a blank canvas (Elkins, 2000). An evocative inquirer can equally create something that comes alive through their artistic vision.

Evocative writing allows us to question and broaden our understanding by casting light on our coloured lenses. Goodall (2005) depicts the different hues of this lens, suggesting that "complex, authentic communication is a rare achievement, [as] people are deeply flawed . . . [and] most families are inherently dysfunctional" (p. 508). He illustrates how our perceptions can become skewed as they are governed by family cultures that are shaped by unique social systems. Goodall (2005) provides an example through the family secrets he inherits from his parents, who manage to successfully cover up his father's identity as a secret service agent. His struggles to uncover that the *truth* equips him with the skills to look beyond the literal and he learns how words can construct, alter, or dissolve meaning, to perpetuate narrow "cultural myths" (p. 5). His experiences of untangling distorted communication systems help him to decipher the silences that hold despair and maintain pretense, as well as to hone his sensitivity for hidden *truth*. This allows him to break free from shame-based narratives to develop a greater compassion for human fallibility. Goodall (2005) reveals how we can enhance our ability to decipher the *truth* by developing our aesthetic intelligence.

Holding onto faith

In the early stages of my academic career, I yearned to master the secrets of prolific academic writers who embodied a tone of authority and knowledgeability. I read their reputable academic papers with the intent to conform, despite dreading the ways that my words became lifeless and anonymous objects (Dewsbury, 2014). I was in a "deep funk" as my superficial and inauthentic lens on academic writing made my papers sound "restrictive . . . untruthful, inauthentic" to myself and other readers (Suchan, 2004, pp. 308–309). After a few years of attempting to mimic the words of others, I finally lost my drive to write. My publication record remained fledging as I wrote half-heartedly, doubting myself and my work. Neither here nor there, my words failed to have any impact.

These years of stumbling around were not a complete loss. They taught me that self-doubt or a lack of conviction could become a divisive force that scattered energy into multiple directions (Merton, 1992). My half-hearted writing attempts painfully revealed how divided motives could lead to scattered and ineffectual results, as without focus, I became a swinging pendulum that swung madly back and forth. I swayed on the spot without making any forward progress, unsure of which direction to take. Walsh and Vaughan (1993) likewise explain how our minds are predominantly in disarray, stating, "in our usual constrained state of mind, awareness and perception are insensitive and impaired; fragmented by attention instability, coloured by clouding emotions, and distorted by scattered desire" (p. 50). They affirm that fragmented concentration and desire detracts from our power, as intent quickly becomes overwhelmed. By dispelling the belief that there is only *one* right way to write, academic writers can let go of their self-doubts and harness the energy of wholehearted intent. Concentrated intent unifies rhythms into a singular motion that is powerful enough to drive the writer and reader into new understandings. Our powers of persuasion are enhanced by the strength of our conviction, as a speaker's power unfolds through "the tautness of the bow-string, this knotting of the muscles, this contraction before the spring, that makes an audience feel – almost see" (Carnegie & Esenwein, 1915/2017, p. 72). Words come alive through the author's strength of conviction and powerful intent.

To write with intent is to hold firm despite the challenges. All rejections are painful, but those involving lived experiences can feel like a rejection of self. I once wrote a paper about a vulnerable moment that was dismissed for being hollow and contrived. My paper was rejected as the reviewer believed that my story had sounded false. My breath became stuck in my throat when reading these words, as I had felt that my *truth* had been negated. I wondered despairingly about how I could ever capture the nuanced mystery of a lived moment so that it felt authentic to another. After the initial bout of disappointment subsided, I was reminded of the challenges of expressing one's *truth*: to write evocatively was to convey words so that others can live them through their own bodies. Crafting such a fine balance was to reveal the beauty that is *truth* buried deep within our words. The desire to master such skill in understanding and expression drew me to evocative forms of academic writing.

Faith is intrinsic to the academic writing journey. Even after you publish a paper that speaks to your heart and soul, the hurdles continue to come: the unthinkable has happened and you have finally published a paper with content so mysterious that it appears to have written itself. Shortly after, however, you notice the data metrics linked to your paper. You click on the Twitter feed and become overwhelmed by the negative responses from strangers who declare that your papers are not *real* research. Similar criticism leads Ellis (2009) to question whether her early autoethnographic writing would be acknowledged as legitimate sociological work. Peck (1978/2008) explains we may provoke particularly negative reactions from others when we bring their worldview in question, as this can feel "frightening, almost overwhelming" (p. 34). He asserts that individuals may "denounce . . . crusade against" what contradicts their own beliefs because they perceive it to be a threat against themselves (p. 34). Such a realisation leads Goodall (2004) to acknowledge how his paper on feng shui and the "American ineffable" could bring discomfort to his academic peers by contradicting their beliefs about legitimate academic inquiry (p. 17). He highlights this tension between the *authoritative* "language of the disciplines" and the *internally persuasive* discourses of creative and intrinsically meaningful inquiry (Bakhtin, 1981, p. 342). To write evocatively is to have the faith and courage to write one's own words and to compassionately witness the possible resistance from others. It is to understand that the greater the challenges, the far richer the rewards.

Writing evocatively is an act of faith as it requires venturing into uncharted territories. Academics take a leap of faith by depicting phenomena through their own rich subjective frames. The prospect of taking this leap can feel daunting as we may doubt our embodied forms of knowing. But when our motive to write for its own sake triumphs, we can become unburdened by the *what ifs* to write whole-heartedly. Dewsbury (2014) explains this difference, commenting, "The will to write stands opposed to the desire to write: it is not an internal, personal, need but an external, institutionalized demand" (p. 148). Courage is required to overcome self-doubt. May (1994) emphasises the value of courage, asserting that it "gives reality to all other virtues and personal values" (p. 13). He uses the French derivative of the word, *coeur*, which means heart, to assert that courage fuels other virtues similar to how the heart pumps blood to the rest of the body. May (1994) declares that without heart or authentic presence, writing becomes mere acts of conformism as courage "make[s] 'being' and 'becoming' possible.

[As] an assertion of the self, a commitment, is essential if the self is to have any reality" (p. 13). Courage is an act of self-affirmation. It allows individuals to "honor and cherish" their own research paths by taking responsibility for it (Morgan, 1998, p. 314). Personal integrity underpins courage, allowing us to fulfil our human destiny to "ultimately design ourselves" and to *author* our words (Yalom, 2002, p. 135). To write courageously and wholeheartedly is to craft words that pulse with authentic presence and life.

The more expressively we imagine, the more expansive our maps become (Eisner, 2006). The breadth of our vision and depth of sight gives us a broader range of tools, whilst a limited and shallow sight generates a poorly constructed map that bears little resemblance. Skilful depictions take place on such an intuitive level. As Webb (1994) explains, "the maker's eye sees the need for variety and balance, for a firmer structure, for a more appropriate form, peering into the interior of the paragraph, looking for coherence, unity and emphasis, to make meaning clear" (p. 163). Aestheticism or *connoisseurship* allows individuals to imaginatively and creatively craft their words so that they can see and feel more and thus broaden their map-making skills (Eisner, 2006). To speak with authenticity, we must enter a similar spirit and be in sympathy with our subject, as Carnegie and Esewein (1915/2017) assert, "when its feeling is you feeling, and you 'feel with it' . . . your enthusiasm is both genuine and contagious" (p. 85). Openness also enriches understanding as *your* maps become *mine* and *my* maps can become *yours*, depending on the mapmaker's skill in crafting their lived experiences. Our maps become fleshed out by encompassing the rich details of another's intimate experiences to reveal endless possible paths.

Writing evocatively requires faith and courage. Evocative writers need to persist through self-doubt, the uncertainty of the unknown and any possible opposition to savour life's mysteries. They must also deepen understanding by transcending superficial barriers and moving forward into the *not yet*. Persistence, despite criticism, can further strengthen beliefs. A rejection can make concrete as *voice* materialises when evocative writers are given the opportunity to justify their approach. Providing a rationale for one's work and pushing back against resistance can sharpen ideas and help individuals *demarcate the territory of their words*. Your voice becomes distinctive by no longer conforming to dominant norms, and like a pebble that rubs against a sandy shoreline, it can take shape by claiming spaces to be heard.

Writing exercises to cultivate faith

1 Uncovering motivations

A strong motivation can help you to pursue non-traditional forms of research in the academy. One of my biggest drivers has been the anticipation of growth and discovery. This desire to uncover hidden meaning gives me the faith to write despite the discomfort of uncertainty. What encourages you to research and write about what you do?

2 Uncovering self-doubts

Do you ever feel self-doubt conveying the value of your academic writing style or your topics of inquiry? If so, what are your main causes of doubt? What helps you continue pursuing such forms of writing despite your uncertainty? Describe an example of a time when you received positive feedback on a paper that you had doubts about. Why did you hold these doubts and how did you feel once you received positive reception for your work?

3 Experiencing rejection

We often write evocatively about our traumatic life experiences to better understand them. Sometimes we may choose to share such writing with our peers through an academic paper. The rejection of such a paper can, however, feel particularly painful because it may feel like a rejection of ourselves. Write about a time that you experienced a rejection of a paper that delved into a vulnerable topic. What happened as a result of that rejection and how did you recover from it? Did this rejection shape your academic writing practices, and if so, how?

4 From the perspective of a reviewer

Evocative inquirers believe that reading and writing are embodied experiences, similar to listening to the rhythms of a song or getting lost in a compelling work of art. As a reviewer, I equally find myself paying attention to the tone and tempo of words to uncover the writer's intent, and intuitively measure a paper's success by the writer's aesthetic craftsmanship. What criteria do you use to reject or to accept a paper? What are some important qualities of an evocatively written academic paper? How do your experiences reviewing papers shape your writing practices?

5 Finding allies

Like many other academic writers, I often feel dejected about my work. Evocative writing is challenging due to its uncertainty, and it is easy to succumb to self-doubt. I maintain faith in my work during such times by thinking about other academic writers who have overcome challenges to forge a similar path. Which academic writers motivate you and help you to persist in writing evocatively in the academy? Write expressively about a paper that you have read that has inspired and motivated you to write creatively and evocatively in the academy.

6 *Take a risk*

All acts of evocative writing are essentially an act of faith. We display faith as we become vulnerable to writing out what we have yet to realise, trusting that we can bridge this gap into the unknown. Taking a risk and venturing into unfamiliar spaces can help you form vibrant new understandings. We take risks by persisting despite our doubts to write vulnerably about topics that are deeply meaningful to us. What would you write about and how would you write it if you knew that you could not fail?

8 Writing in the *here and now*

Just write

The sky is dark and the threat of a storm hangs. People are hurrying about, seeking refuge from the wild weather and trying to get home as quickly as possible. I watch their movements from the calm and still spaces of a restaurant, protected from the chaos outside. My family and I sit amongst many empty tables, marooned on a distant island. "It is quiet this evening," I comment to the restaurant owner who begins clearing away the extra plates. His reply is surprisingly friendly and upbeat. "It is different every day. People may start coming in later this evening. Most days are pretty busy. Normally I start at four in the morning and don't stop until I close up at midnight." His tone is buoyant, despite describing his gruelling days. I admire his bountiful energy. *Where does it come from*? He registers the curious look on my face and speaks again. "The work is hard, but I enjoy it. Imagine if I came into work every day with a sour face? What would be the point of that? What most people don't realise is that . . . " and he pauses for emphasis, "life is fundamentally a game of poker." "What do you mean?" I ask, intrigued. "Everyone is dealt a stack of cards," he continues. "The cards we are dealt cannot be changed, so there is no point waiting around for a better one. We need to play our hand as best as we can. That's all." With that final statement, he leaves me to my thoughts. The room is warm and my body begins to thaw; the hard edges melt away. Thought merges with feeling and an idea starts taking shape.

> Academic inquiry,
> is like a poker game.
> Each person is dealt a particular hand.
> These cards are all that we need,
> to play the game well.
> Our calling lies in playing them,
> fearlessly,
> in the here and now.

DOI: 10.4324/9781003239987-8

His words swirl around in the emptiness as I wait for the food to arrive. My writing has stalled yet again; and as a result, I am waiting for something to unglue me. *A new life. A new brain. A miracle.* The myriad of life's responsibilities sit heavily on my shoulders and helplessness ensues. The work continues to pile up each day and I am nowhere near where I need to be. With academia's relentless pressure for productivity, nothing I do ever appears to be enough. Feeling out of my depth, I wait for the walls of the room to crowd me in. And yet, in the warmth of this small restaurant, the fatigue begins to drain away. The cold wind howls outside but it is warm and bright inside the restaurant, and because it is late, there is no need to rush to another place. *Stop*, I think to myself. *Catch your breath.* Light, weightless, and engulfed in a slower rhythm, the edge of the precipice fades. Understanding sits on the tip of my tongue, revealing the answers that have been staring me in the face. Every moment holds the possibility of a play that can change one's course. These plays involve the cards we are holding in the *now*. Playing these cards is what we are called to do. Because I had not understood these *truths,* the potential within my cards had been lost. I had been wasting my time waiting around for a *better* hand that would never come.

The unknown presents a formidable challenge and opportunity. Challenges arise because the play is only revealed as the game unfolds, which means that decisions need to be made with limited information. Not surprisingly, poker has been described as "a game of incomplete information" because a player's knowledge is confined to the cards they are holding (Konnikova, 2020, para. 6). The play is unknown as it materialises in the *now* through the dynamic interaction between the players in an interlocking system of dynamic energies. This mysterious flow of movement underpins the game, keeping it alive and full of possibility. Similar to a game of poker, evocative forms of inquiry involve constructing a play with incomplete knowledge. Like poker, freedom lies in the incomplete *here,* which contains an infinite number of possibilities or combinations of ideas and words. This uncertainty and openness keep the game alive and dynamic. The cards we hold represent our embodied experiences, and we play our cards well by speaking from them. We make our voices visible through these unfolding plays, which are the steps we take to author our lives. As Greene (2000) relays, we can overcome invisibility by reframing our realities through activities in which "we can choose ourselves" (p. 276). Evocative inquiry forms one such activity where we are free to choose ourselves.

There is no complete picture that shows us where we will end up, and the ensuing uncertainty and self-doubt can paralyse. The restaurant owner's message, however, makes me question this endless waiting that haunts my academic writing career. I sense the futility of this wait, in which I find myself pulled here and there by forces outside myself. These discourses tell me that my ways of knowing are inadequate and that they will never measure up. Seeking to prove myself, but never feeling ready enough to start, is what binds me to this endless wait (Yoo, 2018). The analogy of the poker game shatters this stalemate by revealing that the waiting is not necessary as I already possess everything I need to write well, which is the embodied knowledge that unfolds in the *now*. The restaurant owner's words disclose the senselessness of standing around and wishing for cards that I do not have. His metaphor of the poker game brings light to the agency and calling that lies in playing our cards in the *here*, as these cards are more than enough for us to play well. Indeed, they are all that we will ever need. Konnikova (2020) describes poker as a game that reveals whether we have "an internal or external locus of control, and we are masters of our fates or peons of forces beyond us" (para. 20). This awareness of agency or an internal locus of control determines our success, as she states:

> Do we see ourselves as victims or victors? A victim: the cards went against me. Things are being done to me, things are happening around me, and I am neither to blame nor in control. A victor: I made the correct decision. Sure, the outcome didn't go my way, but I thought correctly under pressure. And that's the skill I can control.
>
> (Konnikova, 2020, para. 20)

We seek external affirmation as we doubt that we will ever be *ready* enough or *good* enough to write our own words but waiting constitutes a barren space where no thoughts can fly. Potential is also dismissed when we flee from the calling to direct our own course. Frank (2001) explains why we may fear such a responsibility, when he reframes the question "what are you waiting for?" into "what are you suffering from in this moment" (p. 354). He explains how uncertainty causes suffering, as to "suffer is to lose your grip. Suffering is expressed in myth as the wound that does not kill but cannot be healed" (p. 355). Frank (2001) describes how he faces this suffering through his recurring cancer diagnosis, stating, "my integrity did not require that I suffered, but it required that if I was to suffer, I encounter my suffering" (p. 359). He encourages us to *encounter* and to meet our suffering head-on despite its "unspeakable and perhaps the incomprehensible" nature, asserting that we commit an even greater offence by trying to explain away our suffering (p. 359). He believes that we are never completely free from suffering and must learn to "balance on the edge of it" to harness its power (pp. 359–361). The wound that cannot be healed for evocative writers is this suffering of uncertainty; we feel it intensely as we plunge into the unknown to write what has yet to come. Our suffering is exacerbated by self-doubt, but our integrity requires us to meet our suffering head on to tap into its creative potential. By moving beyond our self-doubt and suffering, we access the courage to fulfil our calling to author our own words. Suffering further intensifies the richness and beauty of the meaning-making process, as the greater the risk and challenge, the more poignant the act of expression becomes. We embrace this exquisite balancing act between loss and gain to move from what is *known* to the *not yet*.

Suffering can enrich when our losses become gains. The challenges presented by life hardships, for example, may expose us to a breadth and depth of possible emotion so that we can experience the full spectrum of humanity. By tapping into the indomitable and redemptive power of the human spirit, we can also find the imaginative power to transcend our circumstances. To write evocatively is to embrace the suffering generated by the unknown to access its creative power. Softly, softly, we tread, listening to our intuitions, using our intimations to find possibility, and putting down the rule book with its fail-safe formulas. Poulos (2010) relates how we "locate possibility" through writing that is both "dark, nearly despairing" and "sublimely hopeful" of what is possible (p. 54). After conversing with his jazz musician son, he concludes that life, music, and writing is not just about playing the notes but about seeking "all the various meanings" (p. 54). To uncover their various meanings, we must first become open to the fullness of possibility. Poulos (2010) explains how we "trip headlong into an epiphany, or maybe even a full revelation" as we break, and at times, exceed the rules through "unexpected rotations," to transcend the ordinary and "pain, oppression, hardship, grief, suffering," not knowing where we are headed, but stumbling along in the hope of discovering new paths (pp. 55–56). Ecstasy emerges as the smallest film of skin separates suffering from the subliminal.

Trying out a new thought

The metaphor of a poker game connects me to the *new*. A recently retired colleague demonstrated such a tentative step into the unknown as he reflected on his post-retirement future. He had not fully taken the plunge as he was still busily tying up loose ends with his PhD students, but during quieter moments, he would contemplate the loss of a busy and successful academic career. From holding a series of prominent leadership positions, he was relegated to a shared hot desk as an honorary staff member. To come to terms with his own changed reality, he related the story of a friend who had recently suffered a debilitating heart attack. His tentative tone revealed that he was also venturing into the terrain of *new* and unfamiliar. Not only did his friend have to abandon her dream of retiring to her childhood home, but she was entering into a world where she could no longer eat or walk unassisted. She had lost her basic human freedoms and desperately needed to test the waters. *Was it still possible to carve out a meaningful life?* By reflecting on his friend's unfortunate circumstances, my retired colleague was trying to construct a new language to visualise a safe passage into retirement. The unspoken question lingered in the air: How was one to approach life after a whirlwind of relentless productivity?

My retired colleague's dilemma sheds light onto a universal concern. We must enter the *not yet* because we are in the midst of an unfolding story and cannot foretell the future. The ending is unknown and our narratives continue to undergo many unanticipated twists and turns. Understanding remains provisional at best, and our frames continue to be reinterpreted and refashioned as we go along. Despite these challenges, we need to remain steadfast to the belief that the unknown carries the latent potential for rejuvenation. A similar uncertainty leads my colleague to explore new thoughts through the metaphor of his friend's illness. He is unsure of life's value now that familiar measures of *productivity* and the endless trajectory of external accolades have fallen away. His shifting circumstances demonstrate how losses can present a critical opportunity for growth, as we can become fortified by change to attain a poetic vision or a "kind of 're-genre-ation' of our lives" (Randall, 1999, p. 22). Adapting to change deepens the subtlety of our text-making capacities and brings us closer to this timeless essence. Retirement presented such an opportunity for my colleague to review life through a more poetic and embodied lens. His fixed frames of perception could dissolve as he moved from a highly accelerated pace of academic life to a more inner and contemplative one. Such a poetic lens can facilitate the essential and timeless meanings that drive cultural generativity as one person's expansive state can trigger ripples of generative understanding in others. As Manheimer (1999) reflects:

> As finite creatures, we all share a destiny. That common end- the fact that we all die, that life is not endless, is a third element in such an exchange, a "ground of being" on which we all stand. In moments of closeness to the pain, vulnerability, and frailty of others, we can impose an artificial distance, a denial of relatedness, or we can draw near in recognition of belonging to a unity of life.
>
> (p. 101)

Glimmers of my own future appeared as I witnessed my colleague tentatively navigate the *new*. I could sense him stepping out onto the tightrope of the *not yet*, trying to make sense of what was required of him without shying away from the enormity of it. As he spoke about his future, I could sense him getting ready to step out on the rope strung high in the sky, despite knowing that there was no safety net to catch him should he fall. He was willing to take this risk because he realised that this was the path to growth. The vibrations of the *new* emerging within him were provoking similar revelations in me, allowing me to contemplate the hanging rope swaying underneath. His thoughts were setting off sparks of possibility. I began pondering what it meant to step out on this rope and to write without a safety net. I wondered whether this was what it meant to craft vibrant words that could *move*.

So, why write evocatively?

> I have come to absolutely respect the power, mystery, and complexity of writing.
>
> (Richardson, 2001, p. 34)

We write evocatively as this is what is demanded from us. We write to uncover the burdens of our heart, to bring what is *not yet* into the present and to unravel in the *here* and *now*, simply trusting that the play will unfold despite all its uncertainties. We write evocatively because life is intoxicating and mysterious: as Richardson (2001) declares, "I write because I want to find something out" (p. 34). The more we write evocatively, the more we can occupy ineffable worlds that transcend the logical and conscious mind. Lugli (1986) describes this unfolding of expansive awareness as "an intermediate, highly particular state akin to a sort of suspension of the mind between ignorance and enlightenment that marks the end of unknowing and the beginning of knowing" (p. 123). Hooks (2000) relates a similar point, writing:

> We write to find secrets in experience that are obscured from ordinary sight: to uncover hidden coherences in what seems to be a mere jumble of unrelated events and details, and incoherencies in what appears to be strictly ordered; to make transparent what is opaque, and to expose in what seems transparent.
>
> (p. 5)

We write evocatively by "linger[ing] longer at those sites that typically collapse into habitual processes and understandings" to perceive what is *obscured from ordinary sight* (Pearce, 2010, p. 903). Such liminal spaces are loaded with hidden meaning. MacLure (2013) describes this receptivity as a mindset of 'wonder,' as she relates how insights are glimmers of possibility that "animate further thought" even though they may be incompatible with our previous beliefs. Once these glimmers emerge, we can begin to unravel them. Murray (1992) conveys the joys of such receptivity, commenting that he never experiences boredom as he is always observing the world. His alertness and "state of wide-awakeness . . . [and] an attitude of full attention to life" allows him to see what passes others by (Rodgers & Raider-Roth, 2006, p. 268). To write evocatively is to not only to observe widely but to experience deeply, as when our senses are stoked or awakened, they resemble a violin strung so tightly that its vibrations become fully embodied. In this state of perfect tension, the richest sounds can be expressed and heard.

Receptivity and openness reframe definitions of legitimacy and validity around *insider perspective, essence,* and *resonance.* From such a perspective, academic writing becomes a journey of discovery rather than a fulfilment of predetermined outcomes. Empathy and embodied awareness become our goals as we seek to cultivate the "playful invention of self" that lies at the heart of a meaningful engagement with life (Faranda, 2020, p. 66). Life is evoked as we *"feel* the seeds of a work forming within . . . [as] a color or an image or an emotional tone" which may trigger the writing process; it can also be derived from the "startling experience of beauty" found within the world or the search for something that is missing (Faranda, 2020, p. 65). Evocative inquiry consequently finds its purpose by activating rich meaning, since the metaphorical and embodied can trigger new ways of being, feeling, and expression (Meier & Wegener, 2017). Such rich possibilities can trickle down to other aspects of our academic work. Suchan (2004) comments how writing authentically and creatively transformed his teaching practice into a narrative that he authors, rather than a replication of other people's theories, concepts, and models. We write evocatively to create our desired academic career and we engage the "memories emerg[ing] from the focus of our primary intentionalities" to move towards an envisioned future (Hendricks, 2008, p. 111).

By letting go of old maps, we can construct expansive and richly detailed ones, which are nuanced enough to help us navigate vibrant worlds. As Richardson (2001) declares, "What you write about and how you write it, shapes your life" and only you can decide on the purpose and potential of academic writing (p. 36). The suspicion that my maps were superficial and half-drawn helped me to continue re-imagining more vivid possibilities. I sensed that I was only skimming the surface and overlooking academic writing's capacity to "terrify and inspire . . . [and] motivate us toward reflective practice, toward intentional texts, to deeper understandings of how writing words and how we work as writers" (Colyar, 2016, p. 381). Once suspicion was aroused, it mingled with the desire for something more. I desired terror and inspiration to collide to derail the mindless course of my academic writing career.

Engage in the play

Our narrative lens reveals that there are not many 'accidental' outcomes as our past encounters plant the seeds for our future, and without setting out to do so, we engineer our destinies (Randall, 1999). My journey to *Evocative Qualitative Inquiry* has likewise emerged through the seeds planted earlier on in my life. These seeds are a part of my narrative inheritance, as Goodall (2001) explains, "my choice of field is probably also part of my narrative inheritance, part of the personal that comes wrapped in the professional, part of the legacy of our unfinished conversations, my questions about secrets and silences" (p. 6). They embody my yearning for an authentic and intrinsically meaningful academic writing career that continues to evoke growth and life (Suchan, 2004). This promise of growth and generativity binds me to the evocative inquiry approach despite its challenges.

Imagination and faith are required to engage the unknown. The ineffable is seldom seen, but its effects are always felt. They are felt through passing vibrations that disclose hidden vibrance and meaning. To capture what is *felt,* rather than *known,* is to cultivate other modes of vision that encompass the ineffable and honours the "connection between the empirical and the ethereal, between power and spirit" (Goodall, 2001, p. 17). Evocative inquiry unlocks these deep mysteries of essence and resonance, freeing us from the drudgery of functionalism so we can embrace the "fundamental metaphysical essences" of life. As Pallasmaa (2009) declares:

> With age . . . . Every issue, every question, each detail, is so deeply embedded in the mysteries of human existence that often there does not seem to exist a satisfactory answer or response at all . . . . An established professional would hardly stop to ponder questions such as, what is the floor, the window, or the door.
>
> (p. 112)

This chapter brings me to the conclusion of a book that has no proper ending. This book concludes with the understanding that there is no final ending since our scripts can always be rewritten, and by re-envisioning our scripts, we can draw closer to our true purposes. As Pearce (2010) remarks, "hope . . . lives in the spaces between our lived realities and how things could be otherwise" (p. 902). The conversation continues to evolve as seeds of insight are planted in others. Evocative inquiry embodies this generative hope of authenticity, reflexivity, and a liminality of sight that helps us to honour the "beauty and truth" of life (Gorman, 2018, p. 3).

> Evocative academic writers,
> craft resonating words that unfold,
> dynamically,
> in the *here and now*.

> Their plays are,
> soulful and timeless expressions,
> animated by the senses,
> embodying the fullness of lived experience.

> The path of evocative inquiry,
> involves engaging in vibrant play,
> and embracing the gift of life.

Activities for writing in the here and now

1 The here and now

Spend some time free writing about the *here and now*. What thoughts come to mind? How could you construct an academic paper out of the writing that emerges from the *here and now*? Think about the specific steps you need to take. What metaphors can you use to structure your paper? For example, refer to the metaphor of the poker game used to frame this final chapter on writing in the *here and now*.

2 Evoking a moment

After the end of a busy day, spend a few minutes recollecting one particularly memorable encounter. Paint a detailed picture of this moment, relaying how it feels in your body through the senses of touch, taste, hearing, smell, or sight. Shape this text so that its form captures the rhythm of its emotional content. Embody the 'workmanship of risk' and experiment freely with the use of sentence structure, language, and punctuation. Return to your writing after a few days to reflect on the mood that has been crafted.

3 Keeping the end in sight

Forecasting the *end* may be a good way to motivate yourself to do what matters most. Imagine that your retirement is looming, and you have a little over a year before you leave academia. What kind of writing and research would you do in this precious time? What steps do you need to take to engage in such writing? Use these reflections as the basis of a paper on the forms of academic writing and inquiry that you value.

4 *Writing the* not yet

Venturing into the unknown and getting out of your comfort zone can feel both frightening and exhilarating, but when we take a risk, the unforeseen can emerge. Write expressively about a paper that you wrote which took you out of your comfort zone. What did you write about and how did you write it? How did it impact your beliefs about academic writing?

5 *Uncovering voice*

As academic writers, we may derive comfort from adopting a third-person voice and by adding numerous citations. Such actions, however, can prevent us from hearing our voice speaking through our words. Find some examples of papers that take a 'risk' by not relying on the voices of others to speak for them. What impact does the reduced number of citations have? How else does the writer cultivate a sense of veracity? It may be difficult at first but try to limit the number of references that you add to your academic papers. You may find that your ideas flow more naturally and that you can better flesh out your ideas. Reflect on this experience of writing a paper that contains fewer academic references.

6 *Riding the generative tide*

Our academic writing is shaped by the models that we acquire through our reading. To widen the scope of our writing, we need to broaden the range of texts we read (including both non-fiction and fiction) across diverse disciplines and genres. This will expose you to other sense-making approaches. Find an example of an academic text outside your discipline that is written in an innovative and aesthetic style. Underline the passages that resonate with you and write expressively about the impact that these passages have. As you write, emulate some of the stylistic techniques that you have observed.

7 *Using different artistic mediums to explore metaphors*

Think about a metaphor for writing and inquiry that resonates with you. Grab your art supplies and create a visual representation of this metaphor. This should be a physical representation, whether it be a drawing, painting, collage, or digital art that represents the forms of inquiry that you desire. Describe how you felt and the insights that emerged through the process of crafting it.

8 *If your paper was . . .*

Reflect on an academic paper that you are currently writing. What adjectives and verbs would you use to describe it? If your paper was a piece of music, what would it sound like? If it could dance, how would it move?

9 *Unlearning and letting go*

The path to evocative inquiry often requires unlearning formal academic writing training that objectifies our thoughts and discounts our embodied and affective ways of knowing. What are some practices that you need to let go of to write and inquire in evocative ways?

10 *Tracing out a map*

When I first set out to write a book about qualitative inquiry, I had not understood that the *evocative* had been the main current driving the papers that I had written. Through the process of composing *Evocative Qualitative Inquiry*, this theme gradually emerged. Think about the papers that you have written in the past few years and write down their main themes on a separate post-it note. Collate similar post-it notes together and see if you can see a pattern emerging. Write expressively about the themes that surface to see whether you can find an underlying message that ties them all together.

11 *Final thoughts*

An activity in the first chapter involved reflecting on the word 'evocative.' Revisit this reflection to see whether your thoughts about evocative inquiry have changed if at all. What new thoughts have emerged about academic research that evokes? Do you consider yourself to be an evocative academic writer? Why or why not? What feelings, thoughts, or actions do you hope to *evoke* through your work?

References

Allan, D. (2007). Art, time and metamorphosis. In J. L. Jan & P. Wylie (Eds.), *Art and time*, (pp. 1–12). North Melbourne, VIC: Australian Scholarly Publishing Pty Ltd.

Altor, A., & Schildt, G. (Ed.). (1998). *Alvar Aalto in his own words*. New York: Rizzoli International Publications.

Altrichter, H., Posch, P., & Somekh, B. (1993). *Teachers investigate their work: An introduction to the methods of action research*. London: Routledge.

Andrews, M. (2012). Unexpecting age. *Journal of Aging Studies, 26(4)*, 386–393.

Arnheim, R. (1978). On the late style of life and art. *Michigan Quarterly Review*, 149–156. Retrieved from http://hdl.handle.net/2027/spo.act2080.0017.002:06

Badley, G. (2016). Blue-collar writing for fruitful dialogue? *Qualitative Inquiry, 22(6)*, 510–517.

Bakhtin, M. M. (1981). *The dialogic imagination: Four essays*. Austin: University of Texas Press.

Bakhtin, M. M. (1990). *Art and answerability: Early philosophical essays* (V. Liapunov, Trans.). Austin: University of Texas Press.

Ball, S. J. (2012). Performativity, commodification and commitment: An I-spy guide to the neoliberal university. *British Journal of Educational Studies, 60(1)*, 17–28.

Banerjee, M., Wohlmann, A., & Dahm, R. (2017). Living autobiographically: Concepts of aging and artistic expression in painting and modern dance. *Journal of Aging Studies, 40*, 8–15.

Barone, T., & Eisner, E. (2012). *Arts based research*. SAGE Publications, Inc. www-doi-org.ezproxy.lib.uts.edu.au/10.4135/9781452230627

Berger, J. (1977). *Ways of Seeing*. London: British Broadcasting Corporation and Penguin Books.

Bhattacharya, K. (2016). The vulnerable academic: Personal narratives and strategic de/colonizing of academic structures. *Qualitative Inquiry, 22(5)*, 309–321.

Bochner, A. P. (1997). It's about time: Narrative and the divided self. *Qualitative Inquiry, 3(4)*, 418–438.

Bochner, A. P. (2000). Criteria against ourselves. *Qualitative Inquiry, 6(2)*, 266 (272).

Bochner, A. P. (2009). Vulnerable medicine. *Journal of Applied Communication Research, 37(2)*, 159–166.

Bochner, A. P., & Ellis, C. (2002). Autoethnography, Personal Narrative, Reflexivity. In N. K. Denzin &Y. S. Lincoln (Eds.), *Handbook of qualitative research* (pp. 733–768). Thousand Oaks, CA: Sage.

Bochner, A. P., & Ellis, C. (2016). *Evocative autoethnography: Writing lives and telling stories*. Walnut Creek, CA: Left Coast Press.

Bridges-Rhoads, S., Hughes, E. H., & Cleave, V. J. (2018). Readings that rock our worlds. *Qualitative Inquiry, 24(10)*, 817–837.

Bruner, J. (1990). *Acts of meaning*. London: Harvard University Press.

Buber, M. (1958). *I and Thou*. New York: Charles Scribner's Sons.

Burns, M. (2003). Interviewing: Embodied communication. *Feminism and Psychology, 13(2)*, 229–236.

Carnegie, D., & Esenwein, J. B. (1915/2017). *The art of public speaking*. New York: Ixia Press.

Cavell, S. (1994). *A pitch of philosophy: Autobiographical exercise*. Cambridge: Harvard University Press.

Chabot, B. (1985). Understanding interpretive situations. In C. R. Cooper (Eds.), *Researching response to literature and the teaching of literature: Points of departure* (pp. 22–32). Norwood, NJ: Ablex Publishing.

Charon, R. (2005). Narrative medicine: Attention, representation, affiliation. *Narrative, 13(3)*, 261–270.

Chekov, A. (1924). *Letters on the short story, the drama and other literary topics* (L. S. Friedland, Ed.). New York: Minton, Balch.

Cixous, H. (1976). The laugh of the Medusa. *Signs, 1(4)*, 875–893.

Cixous, H. (1993). *Three steps on the ladder of writing* (S. Cornell & S. Sellers, Trans.). New York: Columbia University Press.

Cixous, H. (2005). *Stigmata* (Foreword Jacques Derrida). London, England: Routledge Classics. (Original work published 1998).

Clandinin, D. J., & Connelly, F. M. (1988). *Teachers as curriculum planners: Narratives of experience*. New York: Teachers College Press.

Clandinin, D. J., & Connelly, F. M. (2002). *Narrative inquiry: Expression and story in qualitative research*. San Fransisco: Jossey- Bass Publishers.

Clough, P. (1996). 'Against fathers and sons': The mutual construction of self, story and special educational needs. *Disability & Society, 11(1)*, 71–82.

Cloutier, C. (2016). How I write: An inquiry into the writing practices of academics. *Journal of Management Inquiry, 25(10)*, 69–84.

Coffey, J. (2012). *Bodies, health and gender: Exploring body work practices with Deleuze*. Youth Research Centre, Melbourne Graduate School of Education, The University of Melbourne. Retrieved from http://web.education.unimelb.edu.au/yrc/linked_documents/YRC_research_report_34.pdf

Colapinto, J. (2015, January 19). The day my voice broke: What an injury taught me about the power of speech. *The Guardian*. https://www.theguardian.com/music/2021/jan/19/vocal-polyps-injury-singing-john-colapinto-steven-zeitels

Coles, R. (1989). *The call of stories: Teaching and the moral imagination.* Boston: Houghton Mifflin.

Colyar, J. (2009). Becoming writing, becoming writers. *Qualitative Inquiry, 15(2),* 421–436.

Colyar, J. (2016). Reflections on writing and autoethnography. In S. Holman Jones, T. E. Adams, & C. Ellis (Eds.), *Handbook of autoethnography* (pp. 363–383). New York: Routledge.

Csikszentmihalyi, M. (1990). *Flow: The psychology of optimal experience.* New York: Harper & Row.

Cunliffe, A. L. (2002). Social poetics as management inquiry: A dialogical approach. *Journal of Management Inquiry, 11(2),* 128–146.

Damasio, A. (2000). *The feeling of what happens: Body, emotion and the making of consciousness.* London: Vintage.

Davies, B. (2017). Animating ancestors: From representation to diffraction. *Qualitative Inquiry, 23(4),* 267–275.

Deleuze, G. (1988). *Spinoza: Practical philosophy* (R. Hurley, Trans.). San Francisco: City Lights Books.

de Medeiros, K. D. (2009). Suffering and generativity: Repairing threats to self in old age. *Journal of Aging Studies, 23(2),* 97–102.

Dewsbury, J. D. (2014). Inscribing Thoughts: The animation of an adventure. *Cultural Geographies, 21(1),* 147–152.

Dictionary.com. (n.d.-a). Cadence. In *Dictionary.com.* Retrieved July 7, 2020, from www.dictionary.com/browse/cadence

Dictionary.com. (n.d.-b). Catatonic. In *Dictionary.com.* Retrieved July 25, 2020, from www.dictionary.com/browse/catatonic

Dictionary.com. (n.d.-c). Evoke. In *Dictionary.com.* Retrieved December 16, 2020, from www.dictionary.com/browse/evoke

Dictionary.com. (n.d.-d). Grace. In *Dictionary.com.* Retrieved July 22, 2020, from www.dictionary.com/browse/grace

Dictionary.com (n.d.-e). Ontology. In *Dictionary.com.* Retrieved April 3, 2019, from www.dictionary.com/browse/ontology

Dictionary.com. (n.d.-f). Vibrance. In *Dictionary.com.* Retrieved July 25, 2020, from www.dictionary.com/browse/vibrance

Didion, J. (1976, December 5). *Why I write.* The New York Times Book Review. Retrieved from www.nytimes.com/1976/12/05/archives/why-i-write-why-i-write.html

Eisner, E. W. (1991). *The enlightened eye: Qualitative inquiry and the enhancement of educational practice.* London: Macmillan Publishing Company.

Eisner, E. W. (1997). *Educating artistic vision.* London: Collier Macmillan.

Eisner, E. W. (2002). From episteme to phronesis to artistry in the study and improvement of teaching. *Educational Researcher, 26(6),* 4–10.

Eisner, E. W. (2006). Does arts-based research have a future? *Studies in Art Education, 48(1),* 9–18.

Eisner, E. W. (2012). Art and knowledge. In G. J. Knowles & A. L. Cole (Eds.), *Handbook of the srts in qualitative research: Perspectives, methodologies, examples, and issues* (pp. 1–3). Thousand Oak: SAGE Publications.

Elkins, J. (2000). *What painting is*. London: Routledge.

Ellingson, L. L. (2006). Embodied knowledge: Writing researchers' bodies into qualitative health research. *Qualitative Health Research, 16(2)*, 298–310.

Ellis, C. (2000). Creating criteria: An ethnographic short story. *Qualitative Inquiry, 6(2)*, 272–277.

Ellis, C. (2004). *The ethnographic I: A methodological novel about autoethnography*. Walnut Creek, CA: AltaMira Press.

Ellis, C. (2009). Fighting back or moving on: An autoethnographic response to critics. *International Review of Qualitative Research, 2(3)*, 371–378.

Ellis, C. (2011). Jumping on and off the runaway train of success: Stress and committed intensity in an academic life. *Symbolic Interaction, 34(2)*, 158–173.

Ellis, C., Adams, E. T., & Bochner, A. P. (2011). Autoethnography: An overview. *Historical Social Research, 12(1)*, 273–290.

Elwood, K., Henriksen, D., & Mishra, P. (2017). Finding meaning in flow: A conversation with Susan K. Perry on writing creatively. *TechTrends, 61(3)*, 212–217.

Emerald, E., & Carpenter, L. (2014). The scholar retires: An embodied identity journey. *Qualitative Inquiry, 20(10)*, 1141–1147.

Emerald, E., & Carpenter, C. (2015). Vulnerability and emotions in research: Risks, dilemmas, and doubts. *Qualitative Inquiry, 21(8)*, 741–750.

Faranda, F. (2020). *The fear paradox*. Mango Publishing Group: Coral Gables.

Farnell, B., & Varela, C. R. (2008). The second somatic revolution. *Journal for the Theory of Social Behaviour, 38(3)*, 215–140.

Frank, A. W. (1995). *The wounded storyteller: Body, illness and ethics*. Chicago: University of Chicago Press.

Frank, A. W. (2001). Can we research suffering? *Qualitative Health Research, 11(3)*, 353–362.

Frank, A. W. (2016). Truth telling, companionship, and witness: An agenda for narrative ethics. *Hastings Center Report, 46(3)*, 17–21.

Freedman, D. P., & Holmes, M. S. (2012). *The teacher's body: Embodiment, authority, and identity in the academy*. New York: State University of New York Press.

Freeman, R., & Le Rossignol, K. (2015). Disruption and resonance in the personal essay. *New writing: The international journal for the practice and theory of creative writing, 12(3)*, 384–397.

Gershon, W. S. (2020). Reverberations and reverb: Sound possibilities for narrative, creativity, and critique. *Qualitative Inquiry, 26(10)*, 1163–1173.

Goleman, D., & Tarcher, J. P. (1977). *The meditative mind*. Los Angeles: J.P. Tarcher Inc.

Goodall, H. L. (2001). Writing the American ineffable or the mystery and practice of Feng Shui in everyday life. *Qualitative Inquiry, 7(1)*, 3–20.

Goodall, H. L. (2004). Writing the American ineffable, or the mystery and practice of Feng Shui in everyday life. *Qualitative Inquiry, 7(1)*, 3–20.

Goodall, H. L. (2005). Narrative inheritance: A nuclear family with toxic secrets. *Qualitative Inquiry, 4(11)*, 492–513.

Goodall, H. L. (2008). My family secret. *Qualitative Inquiry, 14(7)*, 1305–1308.

Goodman, J. I. (2007). Eurydice rising: Sound and silence perform the body poetic. *New Writing: The International Journal for the Practice and Theory of Creative Writing, 4(2)*, 141–156.

Gorman, G. (2018). This girl is on fire: Seeking a home for the narrative. *Qualitative Inquiry, 25(2)*, 163–165.

Graham, R. (2020). Paying close attention, thinking to some purpose. *New Writing: The International Journal for the Practice and Theory of Creative Writing, 3(17)*, 297–304.

Grams, A. (2001). Learning, aging, and other predicaments. In S. H. McFadden & R. C. Atchley (Eds.), *Aging and the meaning of time: A multidisciplinary exploration* (pp. 99–111). New York, NY: Springer.

Greene, M. (1995). *Releasing the imagination: Essays on education, the arts, and social change*. New York: John Wiley & Sons.

Greene, M. (2000). Reimagining futures: The public school and possibility. *Journal of Curriculum Studies, 32(2)*, 267–280.

Grosz, E. (1994). *Volatile bodies: Toward a corporeal feminism*. Indianapolis: Indiana University Press.

Grosz, E. (2005). *The nick of time: Politics, evolution, and the untimely*. Durham, NC: Duke University Press.

Grudzen, M., & Oberle, P. J. (2001). Discovering the spirit in the rhythm of time. In S. H. McFadden & R. C. Atchley (Eds.), *Aging and the meaning of time: A multidisciplinary exploration* (pp. 171–188). New York, NY: Springer.

Hendricks, R. (2008). Coming of age. *Journal of Aging Studies, 22(2)*, 109–114.

Honore, C. (2004). *In praise of slow: How a worldwide movement is challenging the cult of speed*. Toronto, Ontario, Canada: Random House.

Hooks, b. (2000). Remembered rapture: Dancing with words. *JAC, 20(1)*, 1–8.

Huxley, A. (1959). *Collected essays*. New York: Harper and Brothers.

Ingold, T. (2013). *Making*. London, England: Routledge.

Kaufman, S. (1986). *The ageless self: Sources of meaning in late life*. Madison, WI: The University of Wisconsin Press.

Konnikova, M. (2020, June 28). The game of life: Maria Konnikova on what she's learned from poker. *The Guardian*. Retrieved from www.theguardian.com/lifeandstyle/2020/jun/27/the-game-of-life-maria-konnikova-on-what-she-has-learnt-from-poker

Kotre, J. (1984). *Outliving the self*. Baltimore: Johns Hopkins University Press.

Kotre, J. (1995). Generative outcome. *Journal of Aging Studies, 9(1)*, 33–41.

Langer, E. J. (2005). *On becoming an artist*. New York: Ballantine Books.

Lapadat, J. (2017). Ethics in autoethnography and collaborative autoethnography. *Qualitative Inquiry, 23(8)*, 589–603.

Lawrence-Lightfoot, S., & Davis, J. H. (1997). *The art and science of portraiture*. San Francisco: Jossey-Bass.

Lea, B. (2012). Poetics and poetry. In D. Morley & P. Neilsen (Eds.), *The Cambridge companion to creative writing* (pp. 67–86). Cambridge: Cambridge University Press. doi: 10.1017/CCOL9780521768498.007

Lewis-Beck, M. S., Bryman, A., & Futing Liao, T. (2004). *The SAGE encyclopedia of social science research methods*. Thousand Oaks, CA: Sage Publications, Inc. doi: 10.4135/9781412950589

Lind, H. (2020). The mood of writerly reading. *New Writing: The International Journal for the Practice and Theory of Creative Writing, 17(3)*, 229–243.

Lindauer, M. S. (2005). Literary creativity and physiognomy: Expressiveness in writers, readers, and literature. In S. B. Kaufman & J. C. Kaufman (Eds.), *The Psychology of Creative Writing* (pp. 117–130). Cambridge: Cambridge University Press.

Lindquist, U. C. (2006). *Rowing without oars*. London, England: Hodder & Stoughton.

Lugli, A. (1986). Res. *Inquiry as collection, 12,* 109–124.

MacLure, M. (2013). The wonder of data. *Cultural Studies ↔ Critical Methodologies, 13(4),* 228–232.

Mainemelis, C. (2002). Time and timelessness: Creativity in (and out of) the temporal dimension. *Creativity Research Journal, 14(2),* 227–238.

Manheimer, R. J. (1992). In search of the gerontological self. *Journal of Aging Studies, 6(4),* 319–332.

Manheimer, R. J. (1999). *Map to the end of time: Wayfarings with friends and philosophers.* New York, NY: W.W. Norton & Company.

Manheimer, R. J. (2008). The paradox of beneficial retirement: A journey into the vortex of nothingness. *Journal of Aging, Humanities, and the Arts, 2(2),* 84–98.

Massumi, B. (2002). *Parables for virtual: Movement, affect, sensation.* Durham: Duke University Press.

May, R. (1994). *The courage to create.* London: W.W. Norton & Company Inc.

McKim, E. A., & Randall, W. L. (2007). From psychology to poetics: Aging as a literary process. *Journal of Aging, Humanities, and the Arts, 1(3–4),* 147–158.

Meier, N., & Wegener, C. (2017). Writing with resonance. *Journal of Management Inquiry, 26(2),* 193–201.

Merleau-Ponty, M. (1967). *The structure of behaviour.* Boston: Beacon Press.

Merriam-webster.com. (n.d.-a). Academic. In *Merriam-webster.com.* Retrieved December 15, 2019, from www.merriam-webster.com/dictionary/academic

Merriam-webster.com. (n.d.-b). Academy. In *Merriam-webster.com.* Retrieved December 15, 2019, from www.merriam-webster.com/dictionary/academy

Merriam-webster.com. (n.d.-c). Whole. In Merriam-webster.com . Retrieved November 12, 2019, from www.merriam-webster.com/dictionary/whole

Merriam-webster.com. (n.d.-d). Whole. In *Merriam-webster.com.* Retrieved November 12, 2019, from www.merriam-webster.com/dictionary/whole

Merton, T. (1992). *Learning to love: Exploring solitude and freedom.* San Francisco: Harper San Francisco.

Miller, B. (2012). A braided heart: Shaping the lyric essay. In B. Miller & S. Paolo (Eds.), *Tell it slant* (pp. 34–244). New York, NY: McGraw-Hill.

Miller, W., & Stroh, P. (1994). Learning to thrive on paradox. *Training and Development, 48(9),* 28–39.

Moi, T. (2017). *Revolution of the ordinary: Literary studies after Wittgenstein, Austin, and Cavell.* Chicago/London: The University of Chicago Press.

Morgan, M. (1998). *Mutant message from forever.* New York: Cliff Streets Books.

Murray, D. (1982). Teaching the Other Self: The Writer's First Reader. *College Composition and Communication, 33(2),* 140–147.

Murray, D. (1984). Writing and teaching for surprise. *College English, 46(1),* 1–7.

Murray, D. (1986). One writer's secrets. *College Composition and Communication, 37(2),* 146–153.

Murray, D. (1991). All Writing is Autobiography. *College Composition and Communication, 42(1),* 66–42.

Murray, D. (1992). A writer's habits. *The Writer, 105(1),* 14–17.

Neill, E. (1994). *Unless you be as Little Children.* Brisbane: Bolda-Lok Publishing and Educational Enterprises.

Nicholls, S. (2009). Beyond expressive writing: Evolving models of developmental creative writing. *Journal of Health Psychology, 14(2),* 171–180.

Nikolić, D. (2016). *Ideasthesia and art.* Retrieved from www.danko-nikolic.com/wp-content/uploads/2016/02/Ideasthesia-and-art.pdf

Noriega, M. D. J. (2006). *Timelessness.* Unpublished doctoral dissertation, Pacifica Graduate Institute, Santa Barbara, California.

Norton, S. (2013). Betwixt and between: Creative writing and scholarly expectations. *New Writing: International Journal for the Practice and Theory of Creative Writing, 10(1),* 68–76.

Nye, E. F. (1997). Writing as healing: Writing improves mental health of HIV patients. *Qualitative Inquiry, 3(4),* 439–453.

Pallasmaa, J. (2009). *The thinking hand: Existential and embodied wisdom in architecture.* New York, NY: John Wiley and Sons.

Pallasmaa, J. (2012). *The eyes of the skin: Architecture and the senses.* New York, NY: John Wiley & Sons.

Pallasmaa, J. (2016a). Inhabiting time. *Architectural Design, 86(1),* 50–89.

Pallasmaa, J. (2016b). The sixth sense: The meaning of atmosphere and mood. *Architectural Design, 86(6),* 126–133.

Palmer, P. (1983). *To know as we are known: Education as a spiritual journey.* London: Harper San Francisco.

Pearce, C. (2010). The life of suggestions. *Qualitative Inquiry, 16(10),* 902–908.

Peck, S. (2008). *The road less travelled.* London: Rider. (Original work published 1978).

Pelias, R. J. (2005). Performative writing as scholarship: An apology, an argument, and anecdote. *Cultural Studies ↔ Critical Methodologies, 5(4),* 415–242.

Pelias, R. J. (2011). Writing into position: Strategies for compromising and evaluation. In N. K. Denzin & Y. S. Lincoln (Eds.), *The SAGE handbook of qualitative research* (pp. 659–668). Los Angeles: Sage.

Pelias, R. J. (2016). Writing autoethnography: The personal, poetic, and performative as compositional strategies. In S. H. Jones, T. E. Adams, & C. Ellis (Eds.), *Handbook of autoethnography* (pp. 384–405). New York: Routledge.

Phalen, S. (2015). Making music as embodied dialogue. *Qualitative Inquiry, 21(9),* 787–797.

Polkinghorne, D. (1988). *Narrative knowing and the human sciences.* Albany: State University of New York Press.

Poulos, C. N. (2010). Spirited accidents: An autoethnography of possibility. *Qualitative Inquiry, 16(1),* 49–56.

Pye, D. (1995). *The nature and art of workmanship*. London: The Herbert Press.

Randall, W. (1999). Narrative intelligence and the novelty of our lives. *Journal of Aging Studies, 13(1)*, 11–28.

Rendle-Short, F. (2015). How the question of form in writing creative scholarly works. *New Writing: The International Journal for the Practice and Theory of Creative Writing, 12(1)*, 91–100.

Rendle-Short, F. (2016). Parsing an ethics of seeing: Interrogating the grammar of a creative/critical practice. *New Writing: The International Journal for the Practice and Theory of Creative Writing, 13(2)*, 234–246.

Richardson, L. (1997). *Fields of play: Constructing an academic life*. New Brunswick, NJ: Rutgers University Press.

Richardson, L. (2000). My left hand: Socialization and the interrupted life. *Qualitative Inquiry, 6(4)*, 467–473.

Richardson, L. (2001). Getting personal: Writing-stories. *International Journal of Qualitative Studies in Education, 14(1)*, 33–38.

Richardson, L. (2002a). Writing sociology. *Cultural Studies Critical Methodologies, 2(3)*, 414–422.

Richardson, L. (2002b). Poetic representation of interviews. In J. Gubrium & J. A. Holstein (Eds.), *Handbook of interview research: Context and method* (pp. 877–892). Thousand Oaks: Sage.

Richardson, L. (2011). Hospice 101. *Qualitative Inquiry, 17(2)*, 158–165.

Rilke, R. M. (2004). *Auguste Rodin*. New York, NY: Archipelago Books.

Rinehart, R. (1998). Fictional methods in ethnography: Believability, specks of glass, and Chekov. *Qualitative Inquiry, 4(2)*, 200–224.

Robertson, R., & Hetherington, P. (2018). Essaying images: Image and text in contemporary lyric essays. *New Writing: The International Journal for the Practice and Theory of Creative Writing, 15(3)*, 370–381.

Rodgers, C., & Raider-Roth, M. (2006). Presence in teaching. *Teachers and Teaching: Theory and Practice, 12(3)*, 265–287.

Saldaña, J. (2014). Blue-collar qualitative research: A rant. *Qualitative Inquiry, 20(8)*, 976–980.

Salvo, J. (2020). Slow reading: Reflections on Jasmine Ulmer's 'Writing slow ontology." *Qualitative Inquiry, 26(7)*, 790–797.

Sarton, M. (1985). *Journal of solitude*. London: The Women's Press.

Sartre, J. P. (1993). *The emotions: An outline of a theory*. New York: Carol Publishing Co.

Schutz, A. (1971). Making music together: A study in social relationship. In A. Shultz & A. Brodersen (Eds.), *Collected papers: Studies in social theory* (Vol. 2, pp. 159–178). The Hague, The Netherlands: Martinus Nijhoff.

Sharma, S., Reimer-Kirkham, S., & Cochrane, M. (2009). Practicing the awareness of embodiment in qualitative health research: Methodological reflections. *Qualitative Health Research, 19(11)*, 1642–1650.

Sharp, J. (2009). *Geographies of postcolonialism*. Los Angeles, CA: SAGE.

Siegworth, G. J., & Gregg, M. (2010). An inventory of shimmers. In M. Gregg & G. J. Siegworth (Eds.), *The affect theory reader* (pp. 1–27). London: Duke University Press.

Sontag, S. (1992). *Illness as a metaphor.* New York: St Martin's Press.

Sparkes, A. C. (1996). The fatal flaw: A narrative of the fragile body-self. *Qualitative Inquiry, 2(4)*, 463–494.

Suchan, J. (2004). Writing, authenticity, and knowledge creation: Why I write and you should too. *Journal of Business Communication, 3(41)*, 302–315.

Tangenberg, K., & Kemp, S. (2002). Embodied practice: Claiming the body's experience, agency and knowledge for social work. *Social Work, 47(1)*, 9–18.

Tillett, W. (2018). Deleuze, Bergson, and a document scanner: Investigating duration and perception. *Qualitative Inquiry, 24(7)*, 509–513.

Tillman, L. M. (2009). Body and bulimia revisited: Reflections on 'a secret life.' *Journal of Applied Communication Research, 37(1)*, 98–112.

Todres, L., & Galvin, K. T. (2008). Embodied interpretation: A novel way of evocatively re-presenting meanings in phenomenological research. *Qualitative Research, 8(5)*, 568–583.

Tornstam, L. (1996). Gerotranscendence: A theory about maturing into old age. *Journal of Aging and Identity*, 1(1), 37–50.

Tuinamuana, K., & Yoo, J. (2020). Reading autoethnography: The impact of writing through the body. *The Qualitative Report, 25(4)*, 999–1008.

Ulmer, J. B. (2017). Writing slow ontology. *Qualitative Inquiry, 23(3)*, 201–211.

Underhill, E. (1999). *Concerning the inner life.* Oxford: Oneworld Publications.

van Manen, M. (1997). *Researching lived experience: Human science for an action sensitive pedagogy.* Ontario: The Althouse Press.

van Manen, M. (Ed.). (2002). *Writing in the dark: Phenomenological studies in interpretive inquiry.* London, ON, Canada: Althouse Press.

Vannini, P., & Vannini, A. S. (2020). Artisanal ethnography: Notes on the making of ethnographic craft. *Qualitative Inquiry, 26(7)*, 865–874.

Walsh, R., & Vaughan, F. (1993). *Paths beyond ego: The transpersonal vision.* Los Angeles: The Putnam Publishing Group.

Webb, S. (1994). *The resourceful writer* (3rd ed.). Orlando: Harcourt Brace & Company.

Whyte, D. (1994). *The heart aroused: Poetry and the preservation of soul in corporate America.* New York: Currency Doubleday.

Wikan, U. (1992). Beyond the words: The power of resonance. *American Ethnologist, 19(3)*, 460–482.

Wilcox, H. M. (2009). Embodied ways of knowing, pedagogies, and social justice: Inclusive science and beyond. *Feminist Formations, 21(2)*, 104–120.

Williams, P. (2020). A writer's manifesto: Articulating ways of learning to write well. *New Writing: The International Journal for the Practice and Theory of Creative Writing, 17(1)*, 71–79.

Witherall, C., & Noddings, N. (1991). *Stories lives tell: Narrative and dialogue in education.* New York: Teachers College Press.

Yalom, I. (2002). *The gift of therapy: An open letter to a new generation of therapists and their patients.* New York: HarperCollins Publisher.

Ylijoki, O.-H., & H. Mäntylä. (2003). Conflicting time perspective in academic work. *Time & Society, 12(1)*, 55–78.

Yoo, J. (2017). Writing out on a limb: Integrating the creative and academic writing identity. *New Writing: The International Journal for the Practice and Theory of Creative Writing, 14(3)*, 444–454.

Yoo, J. (2018). A year of writing 'dangerously': A narrative of hope. *New Writing: The International Journal for the Practice and Theory of Creative Writing, 16(3)*, 353–362.

Yoo, J. (2019a). Creating a positive casual academic identity through change and loss. In D. Bottrell & C. Manathunga (Eds.), *Resisting neoliberalism in higher education* (pp. 89–107). Cham, Switzerland: Palgrave Macmillan.

Yoo, J. (2019b). Exploring a timeless academic life. *Qualitative Inquiry, 25(2)*, 192–199.

Yoo, J. (2019c). Creative writing and academic timelessness. *New Writing: The International Journal for the Practice and Theory of Creative Writing, 16(2)*, 148–157.

Yoo, J. (2019d). Abandonment or release: Words that cut through pain. *Qualitative Inquiry, 25(9–10)*, 1101–1105.

Yoo, J. (2019e). A year of writing 'dangerously': A narrative of hope. *New Writing: International Journal for the Practice and Theory of Creative Writing, 16(3)*, 353–362.

Yoo, J. (2020a). My child and his beautiful body. *Qualitative Inquiry, 26(3–4)*, 257–261.

Yoo, J. (2020b). Every second is a life: Ulla-Carin Lindquist's rowing without oars. *Qualitative Inquiry, 26(7)*, 798–805.

Yoo, J. (2020c). Learning to write through an awareness of breath. *Qualitative Inquiry, 26(3–4)*, 400–406.

Yoo, J. (2021a). Imagining the I-You through embodied writing. *Qualitative Inquiry, 27(6)*, 723–726.

Yoo, J. (2021b). Writing creatively to catch flickers of 'truth' and beauty. *New Writing: The International Journal for the Practice and Theory of Creative Writing, 18(1)*, 74–83.

Yoo, J. (2021c). Tracing the immaterial spaces of you. *Qualitative Inquiry, 27(1)*, 64–69.

Yoo, J., & Loch, S. (2016). Learning bodies: What do teachers learn from embodied practice? *Issues in Educational Research, 26(3)*, 528–542.

Index

For Product Safety Concerns and Information please contact our EU
representative GPSR@taylorandfrancis.com
Taylor & Francis Verlag GmbH, Kaufingerstraße 24, 80331 München, Germany